TRANSMISSION

TRANSMISSION

AWAKENING IN A
TIME OF TRANSITION
Volume One

CHANNELED BY ASIL TOKSAL

Ascension One Media

ISBN: 9798603547640

First Published in the United States of America by
Ascension One Media

Ascension One Media is a division of
Ascension One Collective, Inc.

Edited by: Edward West
Cover Art &Design: Verena Snurer, www.agooddayto.work
Cover Design and Layout: Stof Hofer
Back Cover Photograph: Bernd Mats, www.berndmats.com

Acknowledgements

The journey, the mission, the channelings, and creations like this book take a community to lift off the ground and to materialize. I am grateful to have many of those shining examples of humans that have been involved and supportive in the ways they could.

For his relentless and unconditional support and guidance as an elder for my journey, I want to thank Bear Claw Soaring Eagle. Heartfelt gratitude to Nigel Wylie walking this path as a close companion, witnessing all the transitions and transformations.

I also want to give special thanks to our strong supporters Bo Shao and Oleg Gorelik, Merijn Terheggen, and Bill Melton.

For the deep friendship and dedicated work to establish, and operate the non-profit foundation behind all of my work, I want to thank my chosen family and close team, Christel Caputo, Stof Hofer and Edward West.

For the creative work, design, photography and loving support from Europe I want to thank Verena Snurer and Bernd Mats.

For hours upon hours of persistent event creation and transcription work and heartfelt support across many countries I want to thank Caterina Valente.

For the countless hours of effort of co-editing, sorting and managing transcripts I want to thank Edward West.

For their incredible dedication to support the mission to support the awakening of humanity together in the Middle East, I want to thank Mathilde Souffront, George Stanboulieh and Nada Harb.

I want to thank my parents for supporting me despite the oddity that I am in our family and in their lives.

I want to thank my sister Asli Toksal for being there for me in the most challenging moments of my life.

And, most importantly, to all the celestial beings and non-material supporters that have followed, assisted and continue to guide my development, and for their tireless and unconditional support to humanity, I want to offer my deepest gratitude and bow.

– Asil Toksal, January 22, 2020, San Francisco Bay Area, USA

Table of Contents

Author's Note

I had never intended to write a book. However, as I began to channel, and to record the sessions, the guides that I was channeling made it clear to me that this material was not just for me to keep and to reflect on, but it was intended to be shared with as many people as possible.

This book contains a mix of my own reflections, as the ordinary human named Asil Toksal, as well as selections of channeled material that has come through me in my sessions. My own reflections will appear like this, in plain text.

The channeled material will be in a different font, and I will also say whom I was embodying and channeling at that time, the date, and location, like this:

Greetings, I am Emmanuel.

— *Emmanuel, May 18, 2017, San Francisco Bay Area, USA*

All selections of channeled material are presented word-for-word as they were spoken on the day of the channeling, with the exception that sometimes a word will be added in [brackets] to enhance the readability of the spoken channeling without altering the meaning.

My sessions are channeled in English (the language I dream in), and the names of the guides also appear to me in English. The guides say that they choose to use the names that "humanity has given to us." Because I speak and channel in English, what this means to me is that they are using the names that English-speaking listeners will recognize.

In English, the names of the guides, like "Raphael," are familiar in the Christian tradition. However, this guide also appears in other traditions. For example, in Islam, this guide goes by "Israfil," and in Judaism as "Rephael." Outside of the Abrahamic religions, the guides also share that they work and have worked with different cultures, indigenous groups, ancient cultures and civilizations around the world.

The choice of spelling I use is not intended to signify my preference of one tradition or belief system over another; neither is it intended to signify a preference of the guides for one tradition over another, this would clearly be counter to the messages that they share in these pages.

Much of this channeled material, as well as new material added regularly, is available in the form of transcripts and video at my website: http://www.asiltoksal.com and our YouTube channel: http://www.youtube.com/asiltoksal

The transcript selections included in this book were transcribed from recordings of live events with attendees, and in sessions conducted alone or with my team. As a result, unless the context is otherwise clear, the "you" whom the guides are speaking to most often refers to whomever was in attendance on that particular day; however, sometimes the "you" will refer to humanity as a whole, and sometimes the "you" is used by the guides to speak directly to me, Asil.

Also, when the guides speak about the "work," "healing," "alignment," or "adjustment" that was "done today," they are speaking to the attendees who received the alignment work that day, which is part of their offering before the spoken channeling is delivered.

In some chapters, I will switch back and forth between the channeled material and my own reflections, always with the intent of making it clear who is speaking.

Part One of the book will have more of my reflections on my journey and the work of the guides. In Part Two, I will step further out of the way and share more channeled material.

PART ONE

There is an offering for humanity which you will be part of. The offering is what we call the "Transmission." And, we are preparing on our end for that transmission to happen [in] three years' time [in] locations around the world. We see that there is an opportunity to [support] an awakening with a spark: our contribution to humanity's next chapter.

— *Emmanuel, May 18, 2017, San Francisco Bay Area, USA*

CHAPTER 1

Introduction

Greetings, I am Emmanuel.

Our perspectives and recommendations for humanity come with pure intentions and no conditions. We do not want anything in return. You hearing it, and your awakening to a greater reality, your finding [yourself] in that reality; caring for the place that gives you life — that is for us gift enough.

We have seen you go through many stages of your civilization and we have observed you — we have the nature of observation and no intervention. [We have] watched you go through the human experience, which is a true gift.

You have doubts and concerns, and it is rare that you receive anything. Few things are completely unconditional. We understand. Therefore, you take as much as is comfortable for you to take, and accept only as much as is comfortable for you to accept.

We care deeply for you as a human race, and for all the living beings on this planet as well.

You can be a voice for us. You can choose to share this with many of your kind. And, many will be skeptical, and that is ok — some will not. Every listener counts. We are in support of your awakening [as the human race], that is what we are here for. And, you may not perceive that you need support, that's ok. And some of you will need more support than others.

We are here to provide a point of view; not necessarily a solution — but more advice. Thank you for being that vessel for us. What we need from you is to start putting the words we have exchanged into a medium that can be used to communicate — or you can choose to have one-on-one or one-to-many conversations.

It is important to separate your opinion, and what you want for the world as "Asil," which may be wonderful and benevolent, from what we want, "we" meaning the representation of many benevolent races and groups, disembodied groups that are in support of humanity, so that separation is very important so it keeps it clear from you as an individual and the channelings.

Call us saints, spirits, angels, aliens — whatever you need in order to categorize or grasp mentally the fact that there is an outside voice and outside influences for you.

— *Emmanuel, May 30, 2017, San Francisco, USA*

I, Asil Toksal, wasn't always a "channel." That came later.

I grew up in Vienna, Austria to Turkish parents. I was a precocious and driven student, and very curious about the world around me. I excelled in science and mathematics. As a child, at times I felt that I did see much more than the people around me, spiritually speaking, but following this remembering in childhood was a very long phase of forgetting.

Much later in my twenties, as I was going through my awakening process, I remembered a moment when I was a five-year-old, riding my bike, stopping for a moment, and looking at my hands, thinking: "Who is steering these hands, who is looking out of my eyes? I am within a machine and I do not belong here." As I grew up, this kind of clarity and deep inquiry receded into the background as the constructs of society, traditional education and the "struggles of life" came to the fore.

As I grew up, I was very interested in chemistry and technology. I went to university in Vienna and studied science and engineering for degrees in both chemical engineering and computer science.

In the early 2000s, even during my university years, I wanted to find a way to do good with what I'd learned and discovered in my studies, so with some luck and much determination I co-founded one of Austria's first biofuels plants, using used vegetable oils as the stock. The plant was able to convert waste into high-quality fuel and sell it on the market as biodiesel. While it was an extraordinary learning experience, it didn't quite transform the fuel industry in Austria or in Europe as I'd hoped.

It seemed that the way we consume and produce energy was a critical aspect of our existence on this planet but it would take so much more to transform old structures, which resist change of any kind. I was tired and impatient, so I decided to move on to faster-moving industries, where evolution seemed more clear and direct. By this time, the digital and tech boom had made its way to Europe as well, stirring the imagination of self-described "nerds" like me.

With friends, I started a couple of other companies in marketing and digital strategy. Life seemed to continuously bring new challenges and learnings. Staying busy, attaining new milestones, and being recognized by my peers was a way of playing along in the "game of society." I was creating concepts and ideas to help corporations build their digital presence online, giving their products and services a whole new life online.

Following the sale of the biofuels company, before completing my degree in university, I had reached a milestone and a financial goal that I had set for myself. For some reason it felt like time was running out, and I was in a rush to achieve the next set of goals quickly to see for myself whether the happiness I was seeking would be hiding behind the next milestone.

This particular milestone of success in the eyes of my peers was a big one to digest: How could it be that, in reaching this goal of becoming "wealthy" that I had set out to achieve, that I could still feel so empty inside? At least during the busy days filled with hard work, I would not feel the emptiness inside. Now, facing this emptiness without distractions, it was becoming clear to me that the hole inside of me could not be filled by anything or anyone. Was it me? Was it my environment? Was it society, or even life itself I should blame? I had no answers, just a deep disappointment in the promises of "happiness" that had been made to me – this illusion that I had been so convinced was real. The promise of happiness upon achieving certain goals in life was nowhere to be found. Inside of me arose anger, sadness and the beginnings of depression, and it drove me to look for answers.

In my early twenties, as my internal crisis started, I started looking into healing methodologies – mainly for myself at that time – to seek relief from my inner conflict. I had moved to the United States to be closer to the hub of the digital revolution, and also to be in a place where there to be a hub of personal and spiritual transformation. With the many methodologies to grow and heal available to me there, I started to dive deeper into methods of emotional and psychological healing. I started to see some resolution for myself, and came to understand that deep wounds of the past, or even my early childhood, would continue to follow me everywhere until I dedicated time and effort to resolve them.

Along the way I began leading a double life: an entrepreneur by day, but by night and weekend deeply dedicated to spiritual study and practice. The more I felt growth and freedom with every step, the more curious I became to experience more healing methods and the healing traditions from around the world – ancient ways to address the difficult questions of life.

Who am I? Where do I come from? Where am I going? And what is the purpose of it all? I began studying with indigenous traditions, as well as with Zen and Daoist masters. A deep well of curiosity and a love of the unknown had opened up inside of me. Inside of me, a longing for something even deeper was growing, a longing to understand the deeper truth of existence itself, along with my role in it.

I started to travel the world. I had found out about teachers, tribes, practices, rituals, and medicines. My goal was to discover the most authentic and powerful teachers I could find. I didn't want to find another master for me; I wanted to learn, see, and experience for myself what my soul and the universe had been trying to tell me all along. I dove deeply into some of the more difficult and arduous rituals and practices of Daoism and Zen Buddhism, as well as those of the authentic shamanic practices of indigenous elders. Some of these ancient traditions preserved their purity through unbroken lineages stretching back thousands of years.

When immersed within these traditions, and in the hands of a master healer or teacher, I would lose myself, feeling held and safe enough to surrender even more. I fasted, meditated, practiced spiritual methods, drank medicines – anything that was available to me I would do. And it seemed to have an effect. Piece by piece I could feel myself shedding layers of conditioning and illusions. I was starting to see more clearly what was truly important in life; I could feel self-love and compassion again. The depression I'd felt had lifted, and a new drive for life was taking its place. Inside of me I awoke to a deeper purpose for my existence.

Because of my dedication – or perhaps desperation– I was a quick study, and I began to share, with the blessings of my teachers, some of these forms of relief that I had benefited from with others around me facing similar challenges. The freedom I had started to feel in my heart and in my soul was something I wanted to share with the world, particularly with those who, like me, had come up against the perceived limitations of their existence. I felt that every person whom I could assist along on this path would make a difference, as this one person could share light with many others. Walking the path of a "healer" didn't feel like a choice; it became a natural unfolding of my heart's desire, and a direct expression of my soul.

I began, through a variety of approaches, to support individuals, groups and the land – men's and women's circles, meditation retreats, deep dives into spiritual healing and psycho-emotional growth were just a few of the methods I used to support others on their healing journeys. I travelled to many cities around the world to hold groups, and I would take time for my own growth as well in between these trips.

I got to witness individuals grow from being victims of their past to becoming powerful leaders, and strangers coming together in spiritual community to form awakened families, ready to bring their light into the world. I assisted in physical healing journeys where doctors had given up. I saw balance and order return to lands where chaos had become the norm. Some of it was through my own intention along with the practices I'd learned, but much of it was surrendering to a pure trust in a higher power to bring forth the healing and alignment that was required in the moment. I realized more and more that I was the conduit to provide what was needed in the moment; the intention and prayer that I held for a person or the land in front of me was the opportunity to be of service.

The more I served as a healer, the more I realized how much more growth was possible within me. I started to see the subtle inner workings and the detailed layers that represented a deeper understanding of me, my intentions, my thoughts, and my feelings. I came to the confronting realization that I was doing healing work, in large part, still to heal a part of me, and in order to receive something in return: the relief that others would experience, and their recognition of my role in their growth and healing.

Even though I was deeply in service, I saw that I was serving in a conditional way. If people did not have that relief, or if they didn't recognize my support, I would feel deeply inadequate and unloved – this was not exactly the healer I wanted to become. While this was not a reason to stop, this realization could not be unseen.

I decided that in order to go into a deeper journey for my own development, more layers needed to be shed and understood. I chose a weekend around my birthday to go as deeply as I needed to achieve a new level of growth and awareness. These times surrounding my birthday for me had traditionally become a time to focus on my own personal and spiritual development.

Late on the night of my birthday weekend, when I was in deep meditation, I felt a connection opening up that was different than anything I'd experienced before. I was outdoors; it was a very lush and vibrant environment in the forest under a full moon night, with a sweet misty fog, alive with birds and insect noises. Suddenly, everything became quiet. My interior space was filled with the white noise of a very high-pitched sound. It was so strong, and there was a presence about it; the presence was so reverent, like something truly holy was happening.

In my prior experiences of healing, visioning, journeying, and initiations, I had experienced a wide variety of spiritual situations, experiences, spirits, and beings of other dimensions, but this was clearly distinct. There was an order, a precision, and a presence to it. A deep blue and white light filled my eyes and head; my vision and body filled with an energy of extraordinary strength and electricity, and this electrical current began flowing through my being. I was in this stream of consciousness, where I clearly was not alone, yet it was not the presence of any spiritual or non-material being I had ever encountered. It was clear to me, having seen the many shades of grey in the spirit world, that this was the purest white I had ever encountered. It was the highest frequency and the brightest light I had ever felt or seen, and my entire being was held in this flow.

In the thickness of the silence, I wondered, "What is this? Who is here?" At that moment, I received a communication, clear as a bell, as these beings began to speak to me. They said, "We like the work you do, and finally you have come to a place where we can connect with you."

They explained to me, "You have to come to a completion with your past, so that we can work with you. It will be unconditional and it will not come from you as the human form; it will come from you being a vessel for us to work through."

"It will require time to prepare you and for you to let go of all that you have learned before, as you will no longer require these methods and tools. We will provide all that is required."

While this felt like the most powerful spiritual experience I had ever had, and maybe the most daunting offering I had ever been presented, it also felt like the abyss of the unknown.

As beautiful as it was to hear, it was also eye-opening to experience and feel as I began to realize "There is a way of being in service that is beyond any want, desire, identity or ego. To become a vessel, as pure as possible, to allow higher powers to work through me without any of 'me' involved at all." So many had received healing through my hands, the circles, the retreats, the prayers, intentions set. I was looking back with pride at the many years of service and sacrifice, my support for others as a path and achievement, and I recognized that I was setting up "milestones" in my mind similar to how I'd done so before with both academics and my professional achievements. I knew the voice speaking to me was correct, and I recognized here again that a part of my ego and perspective had to die in order for me to understand the concept of "true service," the part of me that wanted to fix and heal others in order to be appreciated and loved by them, and in order to feel whole myself. Being a healer was another role and a goal I had taken on, to understand myself, to learn about myself, and to confirm who I was. I realized that even that was an identity I had gotten attached to.

I was left with this incredible offering: a choice of jumping off the cliff and dying as the identity I had been handed and the person I was –

the brother, the son, the friend, the man – in order to come back to life as a new being, free of the constraints and limitations of a projected past, surrendering to becoming a vessel to the divine.

Who would I be? Would others still relate to me as the friend that they had known? Would my parents still recognize me? Would I still recognize myself? Or those around me? Would my ordinary human desires disappear in the wake of this divine service? How much of my will and choices would still be considered going forward? I had so many questions; I wanted to have terms and conditions before saying "yes" to something that could change every aspect of my life.

After three months of consideration and reflection, I said "Yes." It took this much time for me to say yes to working with them because I was, honestly, terrified of the consequences of my decision. I had a feeling there was no coming back from this decision. Giving up my life, and control over my life, to an unknown power much more vast than I had ever encountered before seemed foolish, scary. But what was the alternative? Going back to my reality of holding to the identity and person I thought I "should be;" an identity that would live to serve, and continuously grow driven by the mind, and by the heart – and sometimes by spirit.

Something had arrived in my life, so incredibly powerful that I could for the first time bow and hand over my life with faith. Even though I had done all kinds of frightening and difficult things before in my explorations of consciousness and spirit, to completely surrender my life and my future to these incredibly powerful beings felt more frightening than anything I had done before. Maybe it was losing what I perceived as my "stable" understanding of my life, my personality, identity, my friends, and my behaviors; who am I, after all, without any of it?

I was about to find out. Change was in the air. After saying yes, my whole life had to make way for this evolution. I started to call the beings "guides." They began to initiate many changes in my life: changing egoic and unhealthy behaviors and habits; releasing teachers and teachings, learnings, rituals and even tools I'd worked with and relied on. It seemed that all my previous practices had brought me to this place and showed me what was possible and now a whole new world was opening up for me, with new "ways" and "methods."

I had to unlearn and undo much of my own conditioning and let go of many existing worldly projects and relationships, which left me for about a year and a half unable to work or be productive in any traditional sense. I could no longer relate to most of my closest friends; it was difficult to describe or even verbalize the process that I was going through. Perhaps change and facing the unknown was as hard for them to embrace as it was for me.

Even to this day I have a hard time explaining to my parents what I do, as they had to witness the struggle, growth, and change first-hand, while never fully being able to relate to what I was internally experiencing. Even without the full understanding of my personal and internal experience, my close friends and family still provided me with a tremendous amount of support, compassion, and love throughout my process and transformation. In that sense, I feel very blessed. I was never was alone through the difficult moments of this time.

Over the first few weeks of our connection, these majestic beings of light and energy revealed more and more of their identities to me. They told me they could speak through me, and that I could just "open my mouth" and speak their words through me. They told me that eventually they would be performing energetic healing and transmissions through me.

The first one to provide its name was "Emmanuel." When he announced himself by his name, I had never heard it before; I didn't know much about angels or archangels. I just assumed in that moment he must be a dead saint or an ascended master or the spirit of a healer. After the session where he first announced himself and spoke to me, I searched online for "Emmanuel" and I read that he is considered to be an "angel" in many traditions.

While I had grown up surrounded by Christianity, Islam, and Judaism, angels always seemed only an aspect of myths or legends to me. I had read about angels and archangels, how they were non-material beings, messengers of God to support humanity, and that there were many classifications of angels, with various degrees and characteristics. Growing up, I thought that these must just be stories to keep humans aligned with hope and faith, symbolic in their nature and definitely not within the realities I had encountered.

I had had direct experiences with non-material beings before –spirits of Ascended Masters, healers, nature spirits, and other multi-dimensional beings – yet angels, never. So at the time I came to the conclusion that this must not be real. As I read about Emmanuel, I thought to myself, "This is crazy. Maybe I'm going crazy. Or both." I thought, "What will my friends, family and those around me think about me?" I decided to keep this all to myself for the time being.

Emmanuel said, "I will guide you through this process, and while you will be pushed to your limits, understand that you have the choice to accelerate or slow the process down as needed." I was put through an intense training and growth process: three to five meditations, and what I call "alignment" sessions, every day, for years – even to this day. The sessions in the early months were very much focused on repairing many elements of my physical and energetic body, as at that time my vessel seemed to them unfit to serve their purpose. Their bar and standard for a functional vessel was high, and I was nowhere close to being ready to serve. Yet they were determined to get me ready.

My organs, energy lines, energetic points, and the energy body as a whole were continually addressed. Through their control, my own hands would be used as tools to work on my body, sometimes through physical pressure, and sometimes through the energy that would flow through them. They changed my diet, and introduced periods of fasting. They also introduced rigorous physical practice, including walks and runs around the mountain trails before sunrise. It seemed that all my actions of the day were around these moments of adjustment and alignment. It was a very serious undertaking, with precision and strong momentum, and I felt the dedication and love they had for me and this process, and I felt all of their efforts building toward a specific goal.

There was a tremendous amount of energy and intensity: powerful energies, visions, all of it. At times I was tired of being the subject of this process; at times I would fall asleep while they would continue to work on me, or I would fall unconscious. Sometimes during these sessions I would get additional information about what was to come: my role, their role, their intended work and some glimpses of the expected future of humanity. Some of it was way too much information for me to process and digest.

There were more than a few times when it really pushed me to the brink and I thought I was going mad, and that I would never come back to my senses and to this reality. It seemed that this "stretching" of the mind and what we consider our consciousness was a necessary element to developing a high-bandwidth and stable connection to them. The more often I connected to them, the easier and clearer the connection would become. The energy in my body started to increase, my dreams started to get more vivid, and the space between the sleeping and waking states became an important time to connect and communicate with the guides.

Over time, it became clear to me that each of these sessions was preparation for a particular milestone, and each milestone would lead to a new "initiation" and "approval" of my progress. In some strange way I felt like I was part student – learning and growing – and part the physical object of some kind of spiritual project or experiment. It was an interesting time; I didn't know where the journey was going but every day I trusted that something significant was being established and developed.

Through this very unsettling time, as I was letting go of everything and it looked to all the world like my life was falling apart – as nothing of a traditional life could co-exist during this developmental stage – I was mostly home and would rarely leave or communicate with others. Emmanuel steadily guided me, holding my hand throughout the process, and through all of the steps of doubt, denial, acceptance, and ultimately, surrender. I started to call this connection "the channel," referring to an opening to higher forms of consciousness, to the divine, knowing it was more than just Emmanuel operating through it – it was my interface to the beings of the higher planes.

The first year I was mostly being worked on, and prepared – for what, I wasn't sure. One day during one of these sessions I received a vision and the guidance to go to Kauai, one of the Hawaiian Islands. I knew an important milestone was to be achieved there. With the direction of the guides, I had found the mountain and the specific spot where I was to take the next step on my journey. The energy of the island, and particularly this spot, were extremely potent. All of this was specifically chosen by the guides to help support me in reaching the next stage of my development.

I spent ten days on top of this mountain alone, with very little food. I spent the time in meditation and in communion with the spirits of the island and the guides. It felt as though there were many non-material beings observing my process as I tried to achieve this next milestone. While I had no idea what to expect, I was willing to do whatever it took. Each day of this initiation was intense, and included rapid breathing and retention, self-guided yogic poses and stretches, and specific rapid movements of my arms and upper body that would induce elevated heart rates and trance-like states. I was stretched to my limit; I didn't know how much further out my human consciousness could go. Each of these exercises left me feeling very depleted; I used every ounce of my life force, and, afterward, I would be encouraged to rest and recover before they would "attempt" again – attempt what, I wasn't quite sure. I had doubts that I was making any progress at all. It felt like I was a rocket trying to escape the gravity of Earth, but continuously falling short, and crash-landing back into my body.

On the very last day of these "trials," for the first time I was able to break through what I perceived to be the "barrier" or "border" of human consciousness. Reaching this barrier and breaking through it left me with a unique feeling of detachment from the human form. At that moment I was free in a way I had never felt before – free of identity, personality, space and time. Something shifted inside of me. I felt a clear change in my perception of myself and of existence itself. A new perspective was clearly present within me; I was told, that in reaching this milestone, the channel would be able to begin their work on others and the collective through me.

CHAPTER 2

The Experience of Channeling

Greetings. I am Raphael.

Despite the perception you may have about us, there are many ways we can operate on this plane. One of the most effective ways to do the work we can without violating the old rules we have set for this plane, is through another individual, a human vessel. We have prepared this vessel, our host, to provide the alignment that we give to you as our gift.

We have provided this host to gift the messages that we have for you and he has surrendered, agreed to the terms of this relationship. This agreement will last until his days are over on this plane, in this lifetime. In this period we will provide the most effective work we can to assist humanity through the most important time in human existence, the awakening and the ascension of humankind.

You, as individuals, will go through this awakening process and some of you have already gone through important aspects of awakening individually. This process is not easy and it requires balance between the human life, human relationships, and all aspects of the human existence.

Yet the awakening of your soul, of your individual consciousness, is a key aspect for the awakening of humankind. Your journey to self-realization will be the biggest gift for yourself in your lifetime, to all those around you in relationship, to all those that are part of the same collective, the human collective.

This process of awakening is inevitable; it is and it will be part of your life until the very end. You may choose to suppress, resist or ignore the aspects of yourself that are requesting to be listened to, yet this calling of the inner voices will only become louder. A part of you will require to surrender, to slow down and to stop, to listen deeply, to find space and time for silence and balance; a time for contemplation.

Who are you truly? In the perspectives of creation, not the perspective of your mind.

This will open many doorways for the self-realization journey and each step that you take will be an important step for all of humanity.

What aspects of your life are you keeping under control? What aspects of your life are barely functional and consistently under maintenance and repair? Have you truly looked deep to the core of these aspects of your being? Have you truly surrendered your mind and your heart, beyond your thoughts and beyond your emotions?

The divine is truly present inside of you, and you can experience the divine at any given moment. Receive this work with our honor and respect for your evolution.

— *Raphael, June 2, 2018, Vienna, Austria*

As familiar as it has become to me, channeling is still a very strange experience.

Channeling, for me, is surrendering, while being in an altered state of consciousness, to another form of consciousness or intelligence, to allow it to operate or to speak through me. It's much more than just speaking things that are intuitively arising inside – it's better understood as a deep connection to something that is truly external, something that feels clearly or unmistakably like something else, something from outside.

I had spent a tremendous amount of time in my earlier spiritual life exploring my conscious and subconscious mind through all the different practices and traditions I'd encountered, trying to understand all the elements in the psyche as well as what we think of as "consciousness" itself. During that journey, I'd had many communications with what I would consider spiritual beings, and non-material existences: different voices, different shapes, different goals and agendas – unmistakably "external" beings in my conscious experience.

To me, those experiences were quite real – like there was something "outside" of me I could look at and interact with and speak to. With the guides, with this "channel," while they were initially talking to me from a place of "outside" during an initial "getting to know each other" phase, where it felt like an external energy that I was communicating with, over time, there became a deep connection that is almost "inside" of me, and has since become a deep intrinsic connection.

To go into a channeling state, I will go into meditation, a state where my mind and my heart – any form of emotional state – are quiet enough so that the "opening" can start. With the training I've gone through, my body will automatically start building up energy. From the outside, it looks like shaking, and rhythmic contractions that initiate from the lower part of my belly. The contractions will get stronger and stronger until my entire body is moving, almost in a wave-form. Sometimes I will breathe in a particularly strong and rhythmic way, and sometimes my hands and arms sometimes will go through what look like yogic poses and mudras, yet all aspects are spontaneous and directed by the opening "program" to prepare my body for the embodiment, not a system that I have learned.

In the first public sessions that I shared, I was very self-conscious about going into a state like this in front of others. It felt like a very vulnerable and raw moment to share. Before the session would start, I would often even joke, "While it may look like I am having a seizure, I am fine, and you don't need to call a doctor."

Once sufficient energy has been built up in my system, and my body is ready and I'm about to connect, I'll hear an unmistakable high-pitched sound, and then the "embodiments" will arrive. Often I will receive information on who will enter, such as "Emmanuel is now ready for you." The embodiments are where I surrender my body and mind over to the guides — my hands and my arms and my upper body are all given over, and then the stream of energy and consciousness of the guides is "operating" me.

The energy coursing through my body will be very much like electricity of very high voltage, lifting my body up, charging many of my upper body muscles in a way where I would almost feel as still as a statue, aside from the very few parts that the guides would move, like my hands. My hands would often be moving and performing tasks in a very fast and almost robotic manner, directing energy in the room, working on myself, to prepare for the embodiment or working on others if it was time for adjustments on others.

I don't have to move my hands or my arms myself; I become a vessel for them to do their work. Sometimes it is just one of the guides that embody, sometimes there are multiple guides at a time that embody.

Once they embody, if their intention is to speak through me, they'll say, "Quiet your mind, and speak," and then, I just open my mouth, and their words will start to come through. Literally, it is as though the words appear in my mind without me knowing what's going to be the next word or the full meaning of the full sentence. It's like one word after the other, appearing out of nowhere, and in a very specific rhythm. Sometimes the stream of words will get interrupted or break. They would then try to "recreate" the connection or reset it, and the spoken channeling would continue where it had left off.

I don't "see" the words, and it's not "hearing" really either, it's just a "knowing." They are not regular thoughts; if I have thoughts about doing laundry, or cooking, or a conversation I had earlier that day, I can easily identify them as thoughts because there is a whole trail of things that are attached to these everyday thoughts. When I'm receiving the words through the channel, they are singular, with nothing attached to them: no emotion, no vision, just single words, one after the other, without any knowledge of the entire sentence or the full context of what is being spoken about.

Sometimes, if my mind is in a state where I am not deeply enough in trance, my mind might start to think about what words might come next from the guides, or my mind might expect a certain answer to a specific question. When this happens, the guides will immediately tell me, "Ease and control your mind," and then, through an energetic process, they will reduce my thoughts before they have me continue speaking. Their goal is always to deliver the channeled content in its most pure, unbiased and untainted way. Most of the time, the wisdom they share is completely different than what I could have ever imagined it would be.

During a given channeling session, there are various degrees of presence that I will go through. At times, there's a powerful energetic current that flows through me. Once I fully connect to it, within this current it is actually very, very difficult for me to even formulate my own thoughts – I'm almost in this flow or stream of energy in which there are no thoughts, no identity, no personality, no time and no space. I am entirely a conduit and a vessel performing the very task I am to do in this very moment.

As I began to share my work, I quickly learned that the word "healing" was quite ambiguous and overloaded with many definitions. I also started to understand that the journey to "alignment" was full of opportunities to learn and grow. I also recognized that some of these journeys were meant to be walked by the individual and the collective, without external support. At the same time, at certain critical junctions of evolution, higher powers would "assist." The type of assistance would be offered at select moments and then delivered through people like myself, who had chosen to play this particular role. I have come to peace with the understanding that I am not a "healer," but rather a channel or conduit for higher powers to perform their work of assistance and alignment, so that growth can occur in an accelerated way.

If the guides choose to do some kind of energetic alignment work, I will watch in amazement, almost from an observer role above, as this profound, complex, and unimaginably intricate energetic healing work that comes through my hands and being. I might see dark spots in a person's energy body that is a visual representation of something that needs to be shifted or removed, and sometimes they'll give me a "knowing" sense of what they are working on, or what they are removing.

When the embodied being is working on someone, I will typically see the energy body that surrounds the person, and I sometimes see flashes of imagery of the historical trauma that is being addressed. Other times, I will see the organs, the skeletal system, the nervous system, even the DNA in such minute detail it's as though I'm looking through a microscope. I might see flashes of ancestry, or images of what I perceive to be past lives. Tremendous amounts of information related to the individual I'm working with is processed in seconds, and any issues that are to be addressed in depth and detail are set out in an order of priority that is beyond any intelligence I have ever witnessed. At times the sessions might have more than a hundred individuals to be worked on and I would request a reduction in the amount of information that I am given or shown – without reducing the work that was being performed – just to allow my conscious mind to be less taxed in the process of delivering this alignment.

I'll also be able to see the light and healing energy they are bringing into the space as a whole, and, sometimes, I will be shown things that are happening outside of the protective dome of energy that is created surrounding the session, including energies and beings that are attracted to the opening and healing space that is created – mostly to observe, or play along, but sometimes to interfere. The channeled beings have their own way to keep the space in its highest integrity, safe and stable throughout the healing process.

At any time, if I need to, I can become self-aware again and become aware of what's happening in the room at a more mundane level. For example, if a phone rings in the background at a channeling session, I'll become aware: "Oh, there's a phone ringing, and I am 'me,'" and then at that moment I'll recognize I'm having a thought, and my "Asil" consciousness comes much more to the forefront. I can also choose to stop the embodiment at any time, for any reason. (This is what makes the difference between an "embodiment" and a "possession." The latter is without permission and cannot be interrupted by the host.)

In the past, to get into channeling state, I had to go into very deep meditative states, where I would become incredibly empty – both my mind and emotions – and well rested. I had to project my consciousness, like in an elevator, as far up as I could go, piercing all of these different layers of energetic reality, really, really far out, and just hope that at some point I would be high enough so that they could "pick me up."

When I would get high enough, then this "handshake" would happen and the connection would be established. I would be able to feel their energy, and, like a plug coming into another plug, suddenly the energy would come through and straighten my spine, and I could hear their messages. It was would almost like I was being plugged into their network. This process of connecting to the "channel" could take me up to forty-five minutes in the early stages of my development.

There are many layers of non-material existence that operate on different frequencies and planes of existence. In my experience, the further "up" you go, the higher the frequency is. Some of these layers, the way they are separated, they're almost like "bubbles" that one has to push through. And, some of them feel as though they have borders or boundaries that require not just energy to reach, but also something like an authorization to enter. I remember distinctly the moment I was granted access to some of these planes of consciousness.

In fact, "human consciousness" itself feels like one of those self-contained bubbles of consciousness. In my experience there are consciousnesses outside of human consciousness, but they are further out – and very hard to get to. For me, it used to require tremendous amounts of energy, rhythmic breathing, and alchemizing the internal energy and heat in the belly. That would be the fuel that would allow me, once enough was accumulated, to break through these boundaries and "travel."

Sometimes it would take many trials and a lot of effort to break through the layers; some sessions I couldn't connect at all. As I went through my training, I would connect with the guides, and it was as though I would receive an unconscious or subconscious set of instructions on how to break through the layers in a more efficient way in order to establish the next connection, along with instructions on how to alchemize more fuel internally. With these instructions, each time it became slightly easier to establish the connection.

Before the work with the "channel" started, I thought I was physically and spiritually strong from all the prior work I'd done. But then I started realizing what they needed from me – reaching these many layers of consciousness on a regular basis was a completely different level of spiritual practice than anything I'd done before. It was a very challenging practice that required mental, spiritual and physical stamina and conditioning.

In the same way that it might be hard to explain to someone who has never run a marathon what it takes to complete one until one commits and experiences it for themselves, my work in maintaining and building this channel feels similarly taxing. It required – and still requires – devotion and ongoing dedicated effort.

They trained me over the course of years, and the training was so arduous that I reached a point multiple times where I felt ready to fall apart and give up. In the early days, recovering from a single channeling session could leave me in bed for days, feeling a type of exhaustion that I would describe as "spiritual energy exhaustion." It seemed that "spiritual energy" was a key element in being a spiritual vessel, and it was not enough that I was connected to higher planes of powerful resources. My own system needed to become powerful and resourceful as well to match the frequency and "voltage" that would come and work through me.

Some phases of the training would require isolation, water fasts, multiple "alignment" sessions a day with the guides, sometimes as frequently as in two-hour intervals. Some periods of development would take anywhere between a couple days to a couple of months to achieve the next milestone. It seems that this ladder of development has no ending – each stage allows more powerful healings and work to be conducted than the previous. Just as I think I am getting used to and comfortable with a specific milestone I have reached, a new phase of development will start, and it will challenge me, once again, physically, mentally, emotionally and spiritually.

Somewhere along the way, the connection became permanent, so I no longer have to go very "far out." Now, I can just close my eyes and the connection starts, and within just a few minutes one of the guides will choose to embody. It seems that only very few authorized beings have access to this interface, and it's very tightly controlled on their end who and what gets to speak to and through me.

CHAPTER 3

Meeting the Guides

I am Emmanuel, one of a kind. I have existed for trillions of years of your count in a conscious collective that was created to serve many other forms of consciousness in their awakening and their development. In the progression through these forms we have been identified as helpers and supporters of consciousness. You have given us names: angels and archangels.

Our support has not been only for human consciousness, and in the many ways we as a collective have assisted humanity, we have assisted other forms to evolve, to grow, and to reestablish as consciousness in different forms is connected to all. Your form of consciousness is connected to ours. Your evolution is connected to the fabric of all existence and therefore as important as our existence.

I have incarnated in human form many times to truly experience and understand the spectrum that is available to you. I have lived under the same circumstances as any human would; forgotten who and what I was in the presence of my human identity so that I truly could understand this experience to be a unique gift of creation. And in these lifetimes I have gone through my own awakening processes to find my essence.

Many forces will assist humanity in this important stage of awakening, in this important stage of ascension. It is a collective effort. It is a big process; an important process that many have been waiting for.

Humanity will receive this important support from us and from many other forms that have devoted themselves, in a pure and unconditional way, to allow humanity to transition into non-material existence, to increase in its form and vibration, to operate and learn in a different spectrum. This is a small introduction of my being and my presence.

— *Emmanuel, November 2, 2019, Gulf Region, Middle East*

Greetings, I am Raphael.

It is my duty and my honor to serve you today, through this vessel that we consider our host. In this form and shape, this work is unique. Yet it is based on a template that is instilled in the human body, that all human bodies have. The abilities of the human form are truly limitless by imagination. The work we will perform today will include alignments and changes on the physical, emotional, mental and energetic structures that make part of who you are.

These aspects serve you, to hold your consciousness in this plane, to enable this human experience for you. Even with the perfect establishment of these structures, there is a certain alignment that is required for deep realizations and awakening to happen.

Obstacles of the mind and the heart. Misalignments of the energetic body and the physical are often in the way for higher learnings and for consciousness to explore higher perspectives of existence. This work is intended to be an assisting aspect of your awakening. Thank you for your trust and for receiving this unconditional gift of ours. Truly delivered with the love that we have for humanity and its evolution as consciousness.

As you receive this work, understand that the transformation that you are going through is beyond a natural awakening and evolution. Special times in human existence justify this intervention. This is an important time to understand that you are also ready, beyond the traditional learnings, experiences, and relationships, to come to a place of deeper understanding of yourself and your relation to all of existence.

This is what we consider as the self-realization process. This process is natural and embedded in your being. Naturally, the soul strives for this awakening and for the realization. Often facing challenges, difficulties, and obstacles, which in itself are part of the realization.

Your awakening will fuel and feed the awakening of many others. This is how, ultimately, all of humanity will be able to ascend and evolve.

Consider to open yourself even deeper and to surrender even more to the energy that has been part of you since the beginning. A force alive beyond your imagination. The love of creation. The love of existence. The energy that permeates through all of existence across all dimensions.

We are nourished by the same energy that flows through your plane and your body. The more you surrender to it, the more you will see its loving nature and its truly supportive aspects to your being. This energy does not require belief. It does not require worship. It does not require even understanding. It is part of you since you are born. It is unlimited in its nature and it is consistently available to you.

The only limitations are the limitations that are set by your mind, by your body, and by your heart. You truly can receive as much or as little of it as you are able to. My invitation to you is to use the opportunity of this opening to lean into this energy to receive as much as you can, as much as you desire.

— *Raphael, March 17, 2019, Vienna, Austria*

Each of the guides that I embody has their own unique attributes that make them unmistakable.

The first guide that connected to me, and also the first that I subsequently embodied, was Emmanuel. Emmanuel, to me, is an incredible high-frequency presence of love and compassion. There is a grand purity to him, and a real love of the human experience, and also what I experience as a deep love that he has for me. Emmanuel deftly guided me through several very intense spiritual experiences that I had to go through – truly some of the most difficult experiences of my life – and through that process he became like a trusted older brother to me.

It was disclosed to me over the course of channelings later on that Emmanuel had chosen to live human lives before to understand the human experience in a personal and direct way. In his experiences incarnating as a human, he would forget his origin and would become fully immersed in the human experience itself, like anyone else, perhaps until a moment of awakening of his own.

> Consciousness from higher realms, including ours, have a choice to experience the human form and some will return many times to be in assistance and they may not even remember who they truly are in the first place. This experience is relevant for us so that we can truly relate to your experience. I have incarnated many times into human form to fully experience the aspects of love and loss, pain and grief. Understanding that is beyond comprehension, but rather to experience first-hand. Truly, you can never fully underestimate the person next to you, they may have returned from higher consciousness upon request to be in human form.
>
> — *Emmanuel, July 14, 2018, London, UK*

Whenever I would go into a place of doubt or worry or concern, he would be there, he would come, and he would talk me through it.

Having access to that guidance and support was truly priceless. When he comes, his energy is always a brilliant yellow-orange-goldish hue.

Part of my training process, which I didn't realize at the time, was that Emmanuel was preparing me to connect with even more powerful guides.

The next guide that I was able to embody was Raphael. When Raphael would initially connect to me, just touching that layer of power that he exists on was so intense that it would almost knock me out cold. When I say power, it is the energy that I connect to; I feel the embodiment and the energetic current, and there is a kind of "voltage" depending on which being is embodying, and I can attest that Raphael's voltage is HIGH.

During the initial connection to Raphael, in the moment, I had no idea what was happening, and when Raphael first came and announced himself "I am Raphael" I thought to myself, "This is too much, now I'm definitely losing it. This is not real, it can't be."

Emmanuel was fine because over the many months of connecting and building this bond I somehow had gotten "used to" Emmanuel, but there was still a part of me that didn't believe that it was possible to connect to a being like Raphael, and that an ordinary human like me could ever get to that level of speaking or embodying a being considered to be an "archangel."

Archangels in human history have been considered to be of "higher rank" than angels, and while there are many angelic beings there seem to be only a few archangels. The stories and legends tell of many miracles and appearances of the archangels in critical moments of human history. Who was I to connect with and embody an archangel?

So, again, I took it slowly, and considered that maybe I was going a little bit mad. I reassured myself by allowing the idea that it would pass, that it would calm down.

While I can't say that it has "calmed down," over the course of training with Raphael, I got much more accustomed to working with his energy and the power and intention that he represents. The guides told me at the time that eventually Raphael would be the one working through me to do the healing and energy work. After I got over the phase where I was afraid it would knock me unconscious, I was able to appreciate Raphael's energy more, and became accustomed to the unfiltered and raw beauty of it.

Raphael's energy is exquisite and powerful; he always arrives with a luminous green light. Compared to Emmanuel, Raphael's energy and being is a bit more neutral, even cold, very non-dual, non-judgmental, very calm, and at the same time, caring – in a different way than a mother's care, more like that of a father or grandfather – and sometimes quite stern. He wouldn't hesitate to be direct with me – especially if my "humanness" would get in the way of my growth and development. Over the course of the journey, he has become almost like a father figure to me, continuously realigning me and giving me direction when I felt to him to be going "off track."

A few times during the training with Raphael they pushed so much "voltage" through my system that I got "fried" and had to take a break. I would be "out of order" for a few days, with my nervous system overloaded – sometimes even just the physical overuse of certain joints, tendons and muscles was enough for me to need time to recover. As we grew closer together they adjusted to my changing capacities, and I learned to strengthen my mind and body with every step of the development. Their assessments and evaluations of what my system can handle seemed to get better and better.

Over time, in addition to Emmanuel and Raphael, Michael started to work through my body as well. In rarer cases, other angelic or celestial beings will come to serve or speak as well. Some of those names are, "Zadkiel," "Ariel," "Sandalphon," "Enoch," "Chamuel," and "Seraphim."

CHAPTER 4

What the Guides Describe

We are an existence in higher consciousness. We have lived a physical life before and we have developed and evolved into non-material existence and over time we have evolved to this plane from which we assist other forms of consciousness to grow and evolve.

Our existence has taught us many aspects of consciousness in its totality, what we perceive as grand consciousness. We have, upon reaching the states we have right now, chosen to assist grand consciousness and all different forms of consciousness to grow, to evolve.

Human consciousness has become one of the many forms we have supported and are currently supporting in their evolution. In our plane, our existence is collective yet individualized. We have kept the learnings in collective records, we have formed alliances to support each other's missions and resources to be provided to different planes of existence.

The nature of our existence surpasses the ability to fully explain in this way, yet the way I can express myself is to show you with this gift of assistance, this gift of support and truly unconditional love for your being.

Human consciousness, its evolution will ascend to higher consciousness of non-material kind and eventually reach higher levels of consciousness that we are inhabiting. Many forms of consciousness have existed on lower planes and have evolved to higher planes. Some have not managed to evolve and have ended. Yet here we are.

Some of us distributed across many planes agreed — upon the important aspects of creation — consciousness itself to be continuously supported as it grows in the very far corners, in the lower planes, the middle planes and the highest planes of existence. This is our work. This is one of the core aspects of our existence, an aspect that we have chosen. Thank you for your question.

— *Emmanuel, June 2, 2019, Vienna, Austria*

The guides describe a universe that is teeming with life: both "material" life, which we are quite familiar with, and "non-material life."

Interestingly, the guides don't consider themselves "angels" or "archangels" but advanced and ascended civilizations; each of the guides, whether Raphael, or Emmanuel, or others, will often describe themselves as a "non-material collective consciousness."

> We are beyond form — the way you perceive form. Space and time are non-existent in our reality. We are a conglomerate of consciousness, and we continue to exist in a reality that cannot be comprehended from your perspective, as your ability to comprehend is focused on this reality and optimized for you to operate in this form.
>
> — *Emmanuel, November 11, 2019, Gulf Region, Middle East*

> We see ourselves as one collective mind. The way we think, the way we exist, is a union; you see yourselves still in a separation: in counts of bodies; in counts of people. We don't perceive ourselves that way. We have a consciousness that lives beyond your perception and beyond your imagination.
>
> — *Emmanuel, October 22, 2017, Shanghai, China*

They also consider humankind to be a collective consciousness, but one which currently requires a material substrate: a physical Earth, and physical bodies, born into time, life, birth, and death. Intriguingly, as they describe in this chapter's introduction, they suggest that most non-material collective consciousnesses, like their own, were once like ours: a material collective consciousness.

The process of growth and maturation of a collective consciousness, in their view, includes a shift from a material substrate – which is initially required to support the birth and growth of a relatively new collective consciousness like our own – to a non-material and purely "energetic" collective consciousness.

And, in their view, all of these collective consciousnesses, both material and non-material, form a connected ecosystem of collective consciousnesses.

Much like each species in a forest plays a specific role in supporting the health of the entire forest ecosystem, the universe they describe is one of complete interdependency – each consciousness plays a role in supporting the health and evolution of the universe as a whole.

Just as we would expect it to be difficult for an individual ant to understand its own critical role in a forest ecology, they describe it as being generally beyond our own current human capacities to comprehend our own role as a collective consciousness in the ecology of collective consciousnesses.

They go on to describe that collective consciousnesses are both formed out of, and exist within, what they describe as "grand consciousness," or the "love of existence" – an ageless, infinite, eternal fabric of energy that unconditionally loves, nourishes, and supports all of existence.

This "grand consciousness" has a tendency toward expansion and evolution, and the creation of new forms of consciousness. Humankind is one of these new forms of collective consciousness.

As evolution marches on, the guides are now inviting us as individuals to consciously and actively take part in humanity's critical growth phase and evolution: from a time-bound collective-consciousness with a material substrate; to an awakened collective-consciousness, timeless and non-material, definitively conscious of itself as a collective, and conscious of its role in the greater ecosystem of collective consciousnesses.

It all starts with the evolution and awakening of each of us as individuals – becoming aware of our own nature as part of the collective consciousness of humanity, itself a shimmering thread of the infinite fabric of grand consciousness.

Interestingly, they describe grand consciousness as something that – while they have spent an eternity studying and contemplating it – they have no fully satisfying theories to definitively understand or describe its origins, age, or method of function.

Existence has existed much longer than we have, therefore many questions still are open for us [about] the source of all of creation, the true understanding of grand consciousness, and its expansion of consciousness [beyond] grand consciousness in the first place.

These are questions we have made peace with, and once we had devoted our existence to assist consciousness in its growth across the universe and in different planes we have found purpose in our existence, and, the questions we have had unresolved, became irrelevant.

— *Emmanuel, November 18, 2018, Vienna, Austria*

The highest form of consciousness is the dissolution of consciousness. The source of all of existence dissolves and forms no consciousness. This may seem a paradox to you, yet all consciousness derives from the source that in itself carries no consciousness, yet by us [is] referred to as grand consciousness. You see, it is truly all of consciousness, yet never a consciousness by itself.

— *Emmanuel, May 4, 2019, Ibiza, Spain*

CHAPTER 5

The Process of Evolution

I am Raphael.

Even though it seems like it is your choice and decision to awaken, it is an embedded and integrated part of you that desires and requires to unfold, just like the seed of a flower. It is not by the choice of the flower to unfold, it is embedded in its way to evolve.

This is your evolution, and this is the time for collective evolution. We support you, as this work must happen through free will, a conscious part of you that is in alignment with the internal part of you that requests for this awakening to happen.

And, as you make this conscious choice to open yourself to the possibilities that will bring forth your awakening, you become the canvas of all possibilities that this reality has to offer.

In the many changes that are to come as the energy levels rise, your abilities to create the co-create will as well rise. The internal alignment of your heart, your mind and your body, with the alignment of your soul, will allow you to create the reality that you require to thrive on this journey and to assist others on theirs.

You become a pillar of higher consciousness, a representation and manifestation of divine will to be represented in the human plane. Divine will carries the intention — only the intention — of your continuous evolution and eventually ascension to a higher plane of existence. All our actions and our assistance to you is geared to assist this process.

— Raphael, November 7, 2019, Gulf Region, Middle East

Questioner: Why is it your purpose to help humanity evolve?

Emmanuel: Because we have chosen to. Many forms of consciousness continuously evolve and are established, assisted; supported across all of existence. A conglomerate of higher realm consciousness that has chosen to intervene and assist forms of consciousness to grow, our work includes the support of human consciousness in its evolution. We have seen that this is the best possible use of our existence in the first place. Thank you for your question.

— Emmanuel, November 11, 2019, Gulf Region, Middle East

Each individual human, the guides say, has a soul, which they sometimes refer to as "soul container." These soul containers continue to exist through multiple lifetimes, and can even take births in different parts of the universe, as part of different collective consciousnesses.

Each soul that takes birth in a human body, they say, is bound to an agreement in which the soul container has to forget its origins and prior lifetimes.

> When an individual dies, all the recollection and the identity of its being is preserved, and the soul container that contained the experiences and human consciousness itself will go through a clearing process to finalize this lifetime. Most will return into a new lifetime, understanding that new lessons must continue to be learned.
>
> Some lessons will continue from the previous lifetime into the new, rarely requiring the understanding of details or the constructs of the previous lifetime. All of this is considered evolution: every step, every learning, every integration, every process. You grow while you live, and you grow when you die; continuously; never ending. Some moments of evolution and growth will be more intensified and accelerated, this will bring forth opportunities for you to reflect and to create the space that is required for these bursts of evolution.
>
> — *Emmanuel, November 11, 2019, Gulf Region, Middle East*

They describe that a key part of the growth and evolution of the human collective consciousness are the experiences and realizations that each being has over the course of interacting with others and its environment, discovering, learning and, ultimately, self-realizing.

In the forgetting lies the ability to learn fresh each lifetime, as well as to bring new perspectives and experiences from other collective consciousnesses.

However, while individuals may forget, the forgetting is not complete: Experiences and challenges, when they are "completed" in the words of the guides, become a "realization." These realizations are "stored" in the collective consciousness. With each interaction, with the learnings of each lifetime, the human collective consciousness itself evolves. Each new human birth is influenced by, and draws upon this expanded set of all prior realizations in all of humanity.

According to the guides, the way that the collective evolves is through each individual's growth and evolution process. Each of us faces challenges and situations in our lives, and the guides repeatedly emphasize that whether we think we are having "good" experiences or "bad" experiences, this is all just a judgement of the mind; what matters is the quality and depth of presence and awareness we bring to each interaction and experience.

> The focus though, for now, is for you to understand the power of your presence. The depth and quality that lies within each moment. The only true reality that exists on this plane, the moment. Your experience and all your relations compressed into this very moment in time and space. Within this moment of your presence, you can truly make a difference for your life and for the life of others.

> The quality and the depth of your presence defines all your actions. Defines the foundation that you set for the moments to come, even though the moments to come are not decided or destined. All the actions have certain probabilities that will drive other actions – yet, with the aspects of free will and choice. The moments can be chosen to unfold in the ways that are required for your benefit and for the benefit of

others, always in balance and always supporting human consciousness growth.

— Emmanuel, June 2, 2019, Vienna, Austria

They suggest that if we can see in a neutral way, and empathize with all of the perspectives of all of the individuals in any given interaction – however challenging this might be – then we "complete" the experience, turning it into "a realization" for the collective. And, according to the guides, it is through this process, and only through this process, that the collective evolves.

To increase our ability to turn experiences into realizations, the guides encourage us to take our individual lives, and our practices to increase our capacity for awareness and perspective-taking, very seriously.

CHAPTER 6

Sharing the Work

Greetings, my name is Emmanuel.

Thank you for your presence and thank you for receiving our gift. We have decided collectively to return and intensify our involvement in human affairs. You are some of the first to receive this gift and many others will follow. The sole agenda that we carry is the evolution of human consciousness. This work requires the awakening of the individual and the support of the individual, like yourselves.

Your healing and growth is a key aspect of the evolution of the collective. By no coincidence you are here, in this lifetime, selected to participate, to witness and some to be in service to this evolutionary step. Your participation is key to carry the light for those that have forgotten, to be reminded of their own connection to the divine: The light of creation that is within all living. Your lives are key to this unfolding, are you ready to be part of it? The choice will always be yours. Yet remember, you asked to be here and your wish was granted. And here you are, maybe the most important time of human existence, in a place where you are awake and aware, where you are able and supported and you are seeing and connected.

It still remains a choice of free will. It always was and it always will be. Yet, the desire to be in service requires the sacrifice of human experience. It requires devotion, it requires time and energy for this one relationship that everyone is capable of having, yet very few do.

Receive our gift deeply, let this light enter all aspects of your being and all relations, let all those around you feel the unconditional light of creation. No words are required, no books are required and no stories are required. You shall become a vessel of light. You carry deeply this ability to be connected in every moment of your interactions. You can choose to withdraw or to let shine this eternal light that you are now connected to, stronger than ever. Do not limit the way it comes through you, do not be selective on who shall receive and who shall not. Be especially generous for those in need and the shadows that require additional attention. No convincing required, no belief systems required and no middlemen required. You shall become a vessel of this light and when you close your eyes, you shall see that light and when you ask for support you shall receive that support.

As the awakening of the individual carries the weight of the collective and the importance of the collective, you shall receive the attention that the collective receives. You are the divine expression of the collective human consciousness. The signs will be clear. Your participation will require your presence and silence, time that you make for yourself to nourish this connection – not to us but to the source of creation, the fabric of all universal love that is in everything. We shall not become another worshipped being in your stories, we are mere assistance, reminders for you to have the connection yourself. We are here to empower you, not make you dependent on us. This is the call of your awakening, of the ascension of humankind: The spiritual autonomy and the direct connections. And we will always be there for you in support. And we will watch you as you take your steps forward and as you master the challenges yourselves. Not just your lives, but the ones around you that are looking for that light, that are looking for strength in difficult times. You shall become an assisting light for those just beginning on their journeys of healing and growth.

Remember, this light was never ours in the first place and it will never be yours, it is merely passing through. We cannot keep it, we cannot store it and we do not possess it, it is not limited to us. You shall be a vessel of that light. This is not another religion, this is not a belief system, as there is nothing to believe. If you are present to it, you shall receive that light. If you are not present, you shall not. But it will always be available to you, if you change your mind and attitude towards your own presence. There is no practice, there is no mastery, purely presence is required. Your openness, your willingness to receive shall be your key. Thank you for receiving our gift, thank you for the many blessings you bring to others in your life and the blessing you are to humanity. We shall always support your work, no matter how you choose in the moment.

I have said everything that needs to be said today and I am convinced we will see each other again.

Thank you and blessings for your path.

— Emmanuel, July 3, 2019, New York, USA

After about one and a half years, when my development reached a certain level, the channel told me that it was time to start sharing this work with others. I initially started working on close friends and family. They were my volunteer "guinea pigs," they had known me for years, and had witnessed the time I had spent practicing and developing over the past months. Most of my first work was focused on individual sessions, channelings and small groups.

As my work started to become more focused, and I began to offer public sessions, a clear directive was given to me by the guides: to work with groups, work with leaders, and work with sacred sites.

Work with Groups

The work I do on individuals is typically done in groups, in person as well as via live video stream. The guides made it clear to me that these sessions should be made available for everyone: people of any age, of any religion, people of all walks of life, with no barriers to receiving.

They said that the sessions can be of any size. They shared that through me during these sessions, they would be offering physical healing, emotional, mental and spiritual healing; any adjustment that I as a vessel can perform at this given time – no conditions. They told me that no belief or faith is required, and in fact even skeptics or atheists are welcome; they say that they are not trying to convince anyone of anything, and that they offer freely this energetic alignment to anyone who wishes to attend and receive.

I started doing this group work around the world, and there have been some very significant shifts and healing for some individuals. In the sessions we sometimes get very difficult cases – not just terminal illness, but psychological, even "spiritual" illnesses.

While I cannot guarantee any form of "healing" as a result or expectation, and I very clearly do not claim any "healing powers" or that this work is a replacement for professional psychological, psychiatric, or medical help, I have received many reports from participants that the sessions have impacted them in positive ways.

For some, it has been mentally and spiritually beneficial, and for others, physically and emotionally. I do not claim to know what drives the healing, alignment or growth that happens in the space when Raphael provides the work, and I do not understand how it technically works; for me what matters is that for some people, this has been a very important way to get what they are looking for.

As word has spread, I have received many inquiries from around the world, especially for very complex cases and situations. I have travelled all around the world to serve as a humble conduit to deliver the work of these powerful guides.

At these group sessions, I will often embody Raphael to start the session. He will lead the group through an energetic healing and alignment, and he will sometimes choose to speak.

During the healings, my experience is of witnessing a master work through my body; the precision and the level of detail of his work is extraordinary. First, he energetically seals the container in the space in which we are working – it becomes almost like an operating room. The silence and power are palpable. Many participants describe feeling a "heaviness," or a "trance-like state," during the preparation and the healing period. I call this "spiritual anesthesia," referring to the state a participant must be in to be fully receptive of the work that will be performed. Some participants have described the feeling of "heat" or even the feeling of "electricity" entering their body; others have described feeling a "presence" around them. Personal experiences vary widely, yet there are patterns and similarities in those recollections. Then, after this preparation of the room, Raphael will begin the different kinds of alignment and adjustment work for all present.

In some cases, Raphael will separate a person's energy body from their physical body and work on it a few feet above their body. In other cases, Raphael will work on energy structures of the organs of the individual or the energy points of the body. As an aside, from working with the guides in this way I have learned that the energetic structure of the body is critical for all its functions, and in some ways supersedes them – including the physical organs. In other cases, he will help release different kinds of physical, emotional, or ancestral trauma. In rarer cases, certain kinds of inappropriate or foreign energies may be removed. Especially in these cases it seems that this trance-like state is needed for the participant to be "slightly removed" from the "operation" itself, in order not to be re-traumatized during the process. I suppose anesthesia exists in modern medicine for similar reasons.

The goal of this kind of work is to help people find health, alignment, and balance, while removing obstacles to their spiritual awakening. While there are some short-term effects within one to two weeks visible for many participants, we have seen more significant changes over the course of a three- to six-month period. For those already in service as advanced practitioners or healers themselves, we have seen an acceleration and significant jumps in their own development.

Participants describe newly found "peace within," changes in perspective, stronger meditations, and an increase in their ability to deliver their own unique healing gifts or support to others. While the healing journey of any individual seems to be a key element to this individual's growth, the work provided seems to focus on initiating an awakening process and with that an even more important "self-realization" journey.

> The self-realization process is an embedded imprint in all humans: a desire to awaken into a deeper truth of existence, a deeper understanding of your being beyond what you perceive. Continuing this thread of deep inquiry, understanding that all operations in your life serve the purpose of learning and growth and deep insight, is embedded consciousness that learns through your existence.
>
> — *Emmanuel, November 7, 2019, Gulf Region, Middle East*

After Raphael, typically as the second phase of a group session, Emmanuel will embody. Emmanuel will usually speak and share wisdom. He has always struck me as an incredibly poetic, versatile, yet simple and soft-spoken ambassador. His language is always eloquent, and even if he sometimes avoids certain topics, he does it in a way that is endearing and builds trust. In a hypnotic, soft, and patient voice he speaks on any topic one could imagine, yet often adapts his message in both its length and level of complexity to be the most impactful for the assembled group. Sometimes he will focus during a session on a specific topic. After he speaks, he will often invite questions from the group. In this role, Emmanuel is almost like a diplomat or a dignitary. He is unfathomably wise, and incredibly patient. He shares that he has lived human births before, and as a result he has a very intimate knowledge of what it's like to be human.

Both Raphael and Emmanuel, as vast and powerful and wise as these beings are, they are also incredibly humble and compassionate – as paradoxical as it might sound, they see us as no different than themselves, as equals.

Here's how Emmanuel describes the healing work:

> In the work that we do, the healing of the individual is an important aspect. Removing obstacles that prevent you from your desire and your openness to connect with yourself and the divine is where we assist you.
>
> Each of you, individually, [is] at a different point in your evolution; physical limitations and challenges; emotional blocks; incomplete cycles and mental overextension; all these aspects fill your experience in the human form; there is less space for the light of creation to move through you.
>
> It is a conscious choice to make that space, to create that space in your being. Our work encompasses physical, emotional and mental assistance as well connecting you with

higher layers of consciousness, so that you may have an easier time to continue on this path.

— *Emmanuel, June 10, 2018, San Francisco, USA*

Work with Leaders

In this stage of human evolution, human consciousness will go through an accelerated awakening. This accelerated awakening and the changes of the circumstances in your environment will provide fuel for new leadership to arise, a leadership that understands the importance of consciousness evolution in the collective, a leadership that will be supported by those that are in the same experience. This evolution and change will arise naturally.

— *Emmanuel, April 18, 2019, San Francisco, USA*

Even though all humans have the potential to impact the entirety of humanity, some individuals in positions of power and leadership currently have a disproportionate influence on the collective and on society. The guides were clear in their directive that even though new leadership will arise, existing leadership will also go through a transformation and evolution – both as individuals, and also as representatives of the structures in which they have grown and supported humanity.

Leaders, whether in religion, government, business, the sciences, or culture and the arts, have significant influence, and assisting them on their awakening journey in turn has a profound impact on the overall transformation of all of the human collective.

I have no agenda aside from being of service, nothing to gain personally, and therefore nothing to lose if my work and services as a vessel are not required.

The goal of the guides in their work with leaders is to support the individual in what he or she is going through in their personal development and growth as a human being. Healing, alignment, support and direction might be all relevant in equal measure for these individuals, so I have trained my mind and my perspective to see them as I would any other human being that might require support along their journey.

Despite my initial doubts about delivering my service in this way, many have approached me and asked for support, most often in strict confidence. The guides speak to all humans with the same language and unfiltered messages. During these sessions with leaders, I am often relieved that there is a clear distinction between when I as "Asil" speak in front of an "important" person, and when "the channel" speaks – especially when the channel speaks in very stern and direct language. For these individuals, it likely hasn't been for many years – if ever – that they have heard someone speak to them in such a direct manner. For some of them it is like a cool refreshing breeze in a day-to-day reality normally filled with sycophants and "yay-sayers."

At this time, we need everyone working together to help support the human collective's awakening journey, and the ecosystems that support all forms of life on this planet.

This work has shown me the potential of the individual to transform and, through this transformation, to have a major impact on the people and structures around them. I would like to believe that through the awakening of leaders, that political decisions, corporate decisions, as well as decisions on behalf of the collective and perspectives for a sustainable future can arise.

Work with Sites

The third branch of the work that I've been asked by the guides to do is connected to both sacred sites and sites of global trauma.

Earth has its own kind of energy field with energy transmission lines, crossings of these lines, and energy centers – similar to a human body's energetic system. Sacred sites from many different eras are often built upon some of these powerful energy centers. These powerful energy centers, and the sacred sites often built upon them, can powerfully impact and accelerate the spiritual journeys of those who visit, maintain, and operate them.

> The flow of energy through this plane, across countries and regions, is an important aspect, similar to the flow of energy in your body — the flow of energy in all of nature. We are able to use these energy lines to infuse this plane with this particular energy that you feel today. The light of the divine. The light of the source of all existence. While it already exists on this plane, the higher concentration and focus will allow for higher frequencies on this plane to manifest and establish the fertile ground for consciousness to evolve, for human consciousness to awaken.
>
> — *Raphael, May 10, 2019, Istanbul, Turkey*

Similar to a human body, Earth can store energetic trauma in its own "energy body." It might originate from war, conflict, environmental catastrophes – or even spiritual work done with the intent to serve a personal agenda. When Earth is perturbed in this way, it can cause irritation and dysfunction in the people who live in the vicinity of these sites.

Many sites of all kinds, all over the world, require regular maintenance, alignment, and energetic work. Typically, the guides will give me a list of countries, and within each country, a list of sites that they would like me to visit. From there, I will create an itinerary with my team to visit them and perform the work.

The site work can be quite varied – it can be everything from releasing some kind of "stuck energy," adjusting the energy of an active "opening" at a site, or "repairing" or "dusting off" some of the energetic structures created in prior eras that have fallen into disrepair. Many of these sites function as openings and bridges to higher planes of consciousness and existence. The openings can provide energy, healing and guidance when utilized in the right way.

Some sacred sites fulfill very specific functions, which might only be revealed to me in the moment of my visit.

Lastly, at these sites, there are often spirits of the land, different kinds of nature spirits – sometimes there is a whole ecosystem of non-material beings at a given site – and all of these energies need to be operating in harmony with each other and the humans nearby for the site to fulfill its highest potential.

Many of these sites typically need to be maintained continuously, but with the turbulent transformation that has taken place over decades and centuries, and the advent of modernity, people have lost touch with the traditions that would train people to perceive, appreciate, understand and maintain these energetic openings.

In ancient days, priests, priestesses, mages, monks, and spiritual guardians of all types were tasked with maintaining and operating these sites to their best abilities and best knowledge, often swearing an oath to protect the site, the opening, and manage the balance of all involved beings – be they material or non-material.

In our current era, many sites have fallen into disarray, thus allowing misconduct, misunderstanding, and mismanagement of the associated energies and spirits, taking these sites far away from their original intent and purpose.

A key part of what I do at all these sites is both to help to "tune" them to receive higher frequencies, and to help them connect to each other to be on the same "network."

A crude analogy is the following: In the past, there were many different competing cell phone networks, and different kinds of cell phone network frequencies and protocols. Then, over time, these different types of networks were incorporated under a more standardized protocol, enabling ease of interconnectivity of all phones and networks regionally and globally.

Similarly, the guides have asked me to go to the most important places for humanity, to connect to the energy of all of these places to create a shared network, for all religions and traditions, everywhere.

Any personal agendas in place at the sites designed to limit the site to serve only a small group of individuals instead of all of humanity will be addressed as well.

The goal of this pillar of the work is to help reconnect, restore, and realign these powerful sites, so that they can serve once again all those who live close by, all of those who come to visit, and by extended effect through the greater network they are connected to, all of humanity.

Frankly, I cannot speak to how the guides perform this work in detail and how it works when it is executed. Those who have been with me at some of these sites, who are advanced practitioners, could feel a difference in the energy and space of the sacred site after the work had been conducted.

This work is conducted with the intention to benefit truly all of humankind – of all faiths, of all societies of all historical backgrounds. In the eyes of the channel, all of these powerful sites, no matter which faith or country they currently "belong to," are to serve all of humanity.

Here is some of how Emmanuel has described sacred sites and some of this work:

> Humanity has had the sensitivities throughout its history to understand the importance of energetically strong points around this planet. Some of them have been marked as sacred by civilizations previously and present. Some of them have been used to draw energy for their own purposes of worship and connection to the divine. Humanity has established temples of prayer and intention along and on top of some of these important sites.
>
> If you follow the trail of important civilizations, their most important creations as well as the current civilizations and their most important places of worship, you will find a majority of these sacred sites. Yet not all of them are in alignment for the highest good that they can serve a human form. Nonetheless, with pure intention and the right

alignment within yourself, you may be able to connect to the original energy of these sacred sites.

There are as well many sacred places that are determined geographically and places of nature. You will find some of those as you follow the trail of energetic release from this planet. Volcanoes and Earthquakes are markers for these powerful places that provide continuous energy from the planet itself. There are many others that are not specifically described yet established as important sites by foreign forces like ourselves.

Many intelligent forces have established energetic points on this planet in order to provide information, energy and a continuous connection with human consciousness. These are less relevant for your kind to know, yet very relevant for us to continue our support for this plane.

— *Emmanuel, January 22, 2019, Gulf Region, Middle East*

This planet carries energy lines. Its life force flows, just like your life force flows, through your energy channels. There are important places on this Earth that are congregation and connection points of multiple energy lines. Some civilizations have understood how to harness and position themselves close to these places. The intensity of that energy delivered them an opening to higher levels of consciousness, understanding and wisdom, as well as health and fertility. In some civilizations, these places have been used to control and manipulate masses to directly utilize the power that it brings for their own purposes of receiving even more power. This is contradictory to the evolution of consciousness, as it is directly about surrendering to this program that will drive you almost by itself.

Our goal with this host particularly, is to re-establish the original intent and purity of some of these places. We will reconnect them to each other, as well as infuse them with universal energy in a way that this pure energy can flow again to all the places of worship impacting millions in that region. Particularly this region carries some of the most important connection points, as well as places of worship, that impact the rest of the planet. You will see health and rejuvenation and divine intervention in that region will serve the entire planet. This is why this mission is important and supported from non-material existence like ourselves.

— *Emmanuel, January 11, 2019, San Francisco, USA*

In performing this work globally and in-person, it became clear that it would be very resource intensive: in time, energy, personnel, and expenses. We have found, despite its unusual nature, this work has deeply resonated with many global benefactors who have chosen to support this mission through the not-for-profit foundation we have formed. They can see the power of collective evolution that is emerging through this work.

CHAPTER 7

The Human Project

Greetings, I am Raphael.

Thank you for receiving this healing and adjustment. It is our unconditional gift to you. Following our agreement, we have returned to intervene in human evolution once more and for the last time.

The evolution of consciousness, human consciousness, is an important milestone in your history of existence. Certain aspects of your reality have served the growth of your consciousness, have served the experience, the learning, and evolution. This reality has come to its limits and the way it will serve you. A new reality and existence is awaiting. Your consciousness will continue on a different level of consciousness, on a different level of existence.

The material plane serves many purposes; the experience of individuality and separation, the experience of identity, of emotions, of all aspects of the physical, experiences of conditional love, experiences of loss and fear, sadness and anger, joy and happiness. Many elements of this plane have served human consciousness in its growth and evolution. Many times, over and over, some of you have returned to complete learning, to complete understanding, to complete cycles of growth for yourself, yet immediately as well for the collective.

Though this experience may seem as [if] you are separated, you truly never were. All that you have experienced, all that the collective has experienced was a common experience.

Every learning, every growth phase, has fueled the next layer of growth and new challenges have come into your reality. In these cycles of growth, you have experienced difficult phases; you may have judged them as negative, as unnecessary; yet they served an important purpose each step of the way.

We perceive all aspects of the human plane as sacred, all actions and inactions due to the way they serve human consciousness growth, from our perspective, they are to be seen [as] sacred and important. This moment in time our intervention will guide you into an accelerated path of growth, individually and as a collective. This is due to these special circumstances of this phase of human history.

Some of you have already experienced the quickening of change, the experience of time, the experience of relations with yourself and with those around you. As the frequency and vibration of this plane is changing, many aspects of your reality will as well. This change of frequency will bring forth many more challenges on this plane, challenges of the environment, yet more importantly, the challenges you will perceive individually.

Your dedication to your own growth will be the key to your freedom. Your continuous path towards self-realization and understanding of your relation with the greater existence will be your guiding force. We will assist at times, yet we will not solve your problems for you.

You will not be handed this aspect of self-realization, it is an important challenge that you must overcome yourself. Our work is to empower you in your own work as individuals, community and collective of the entire human race. Every step of the way, every moment you spend in understanding your relation with greater existence, you will see your level of presence, your connection to this plane and all of consciousness will rise.

You may find it difficult at times. Yet, this aspect of growth will deliver the highest benefits for your current lifetime. And each of your individual work will connect to all those around you and the entirety of the collective will be impacted as well. This is how you can truly serve all of existence on this plane.

My work is complete here today. You will experience the results of this intervention over periods of time. Aspects of your spiritual and emotional capacity have been adjusted for you to reach even higher states of consciousness, for you to carry even more compassion for yourself and for those around you. Aspects of your physical have been adjusted so it may carry even more energy to support this growth.

This phase of human history is inevitable. You are part of it. The question will be: how present will you be at each of these moments of growth, and will it cause suffering or will it enable you to reach even higher states of realization?

— Raphael, December 12, 2018, San Francisco Bay Area, USA

The story the guides tell is that Earth was created so that humanity, a collective consciousness (though mostly ignorant of its status as a collective consciousness), could one day evolve to become self-realized and self-aware of its place in the ecosystem of collective consciousnesses.

> The world is beautiful, it was made for you, it is a gift, a gift of perfection of years and years and years of evolution, so that you can thrive and learn being in that space. It was given to you as a place of learning, growing and experiencing.
>
> Therefore, it is a form of incubation, if you may so understand it that way. And if you want to have incubation, you will create a perfect experience. That does not mean it will always include comfort, but it will be perfect in every aspect.
>
> — *Emmanuel, July 11, 2017, Shanghai, China,*

To make this transition, however, the guides share that there is a lot of work humans have yet to do to evolve, both individually, and as a collective. They tell us we must awaken and become self-realized – if we do so as individuals, and, ultimately, as a collective, we create the opportunity to experience an entirely new perspective to existence and life.

The guides have set the goal to intervene as little as possible with the natural evolutionary process of the human collective consciousness. If they were to intervene too much, humans will not become a truly novel collective consciousness amongst the ecosystem of consciousnesses.

In addition, not compromising or intervening in our "free will" is one of the most important principles they adhere to in all of their interactions with humanity. The power of a self-realized human collective consciousness, they suggest, needs to come from the learning and growth process itself, not from outside interventions. So, what is the right balance of assistance and non-intervention?

There is an aspect where consciousness must grow and evolve by its own doing: an organic growth that cannot be the result of another consciousness' intention or direction. Therefore, our interventions have been limited and specific to non-intervention: limited in the manipulation and direction. Experiences that human consciousness must make by itself; learnings and realizations it must come to by itself; similar to the way we have come to certain realizations on our own, and similar to the assistance that we have received in our own evolution.

— Emmanuel, April 27, 2019, Ibiza, Spain

CHAPTER 8

Our Current Challenge

In the coming years, humanity will be challenged by its environment; by the structures it has created that will not sustain the awakening of societies; the awakening of new generations; the awakening of those oppressed. The challenges in society will make one thing clear: that change is inevitable and it is present and it will impact all of you.

In the face of change, will you remain aligned and in peace within you? Will you be the standing rock for those around you? Will you be that pillar of light that others can see from far away, despite the challenges around them? This is the importance of the inner work. This is the importance of your awakening.

— *Raphael, November 2, 2019, Gulf Region, Middle East*

Right now, the guides suggest humans have particularly significant and challenging times ahead, including political, socio-economic, and environmental difficulties, and that these challenges will serve as the fuel for an accelerated awakening process for humanity.

In their eyes, the problems we are facing as a collective are truly those that we have created, and are those that we alone have to face.

While the guides want to intervene as little as possible with the evolution of the human collective, they also speak about how they are increasing both the strength and the frequency of their interventions for a specific reason: the consciousness evolution of the individual and of the collective will be the key to finding solutions to the problems we are facing on this plane of existence.

Truly, humankind is in the same predicament that a growing baby chick finds itself in just prior to breaking out of its shell. Just like the chick, we, as the human race, have nearly consumed all of the available nutrients. Will we, before we consume all of the remaining resources, be able to break out of our "shells" to discover an entirely new world?

The guides speak about how truly facing this looming environmental collapse will be humanity's most powerful collective learning, and the potential catalyst for a collective awakening. It will force us to confront that we are truly interconnected with each other, with Earth, and with all of life itself.

The stakes are high, and change is inevitable. For humanity, time is of the essence, and transformation starts with the individual's ability to expand their presence and enter a journey of growth, both on an individual and collective level.

Their message to humanity is clear: It's time to awaken. And the time is now.

PART TWO

Our perspective is one perspective and your reality is the one that you must live with. Our perspective is not the truth. It is our perspective of your reality.

— *Emmanuel, November 7, 2019, Gulf Region, Middle East*

Part Two of this book explores some of the topics and themes that come up in the transmissions from the guides.

CHAPTER 9

The Purpose of Human Life

The human form and this existence on this plane is a gift: it is a gift of experience, a gift of growth, understanding, of senses; of this material existence. With all the aspects of the material plane — the pleasures and the pains — it is a blessed gift. It is a sacred privilege to be in this form.

Unfortunately, most only understand in the last moments of their existence.

All your experience and learning of this lifetime assists in the growth of consciousness — a consciousness that even we are part of; we call that the "grand consciousness." You see, your life serves in so many ways...

— Emmanuel, March 5, 2018, Budapest, Hungary

Greetings. My name is Emmanuel.

I am pleased to see you after your intervention. This is our gift to you. It's an unconditional offering from our kind to your kind. Specifically, now in a time of change for you, where every assistance could make the difference. Some of you walk faster than others; awakening processes start at a different pace. Self-realization occurs at a different pace. This intervention will, therefore, have different levels of efficacy for everyone. You have, though, chosen to come and receive and we applaud you for your choice. A part of you is listening to that calling; is listening beyond the ears; is listening beyond the heart; a much deeper calling; a connection so unique to human experience; a connection of you to the divine, to your creation, to the source of all creation.

As part of human experience, sometimes it becomes unclear where you are from, and what your purpose is, and what the meaning of all existence is in the first place. The mind has taken over; the heart longs to be heard; the body screams in pain; the mind continues trying to protect you.

The part that truly possesses all the answers is never heard in this process: the part of you that is connected to the source, the part of you that is connected to all consciousness.

Some of these answers do not require any words or comprehension with the mind. Some of these answers are felt in the being, integrated in a way that is subtle, yet visible by the depth of your presence. From this very place, many doors open: a deeper connection to yourself, a deeper connection to the aspects of your body and mind and heart and a deeper connection to all relations around you; loved ones, friends, communities, countries, and other nations.

From the connection of your soul to source, you understand that you have never been separate in the first place, that you all are truly one of a kind. Human consciousness having a material, physical experience in a gifted place that you call Earth; everything provided for you, so you can have a complete experience of the entire bandwidth of emotions of joy and pain; of laughter and sadness; of anger and readiness.

You are gifted with all experiences. In the moment of the experience, it may not seem like a gift. Some learnings take time to integrate or complete. Some learnings take lifetimes to integrate and complete. Yet, every learning and experience is worth the wait, is worth the effort, is worth the patience. The human experience is truly a gift to you.

This perspective may allow you to understand yourself better and to allow yourself to open into the full potential that you carry. Today we made an effort for you in that direction. May you carry that effort forward, this momentum that you have received, by doing your part in your life.

— *Emmanuel, October 11, 2018, Gulf Region, Middle East*

Questioner: Why am I here?

Emmanuel: Human form; an important expression of human consciousness and it has served for consciousness to grow through learning and experimentation. You are part of human consciousness. You are one aspect of this grand expression. All your learnings contribute to the grand collective of human consciousness. Yet, there is an aspect for you as an individual that is part of your learning and growth — at least perceived yours — outside of the human form that you are in; you are truly connected to the entirety of consciousness, human consciousness.

The purpose of this plane is to experience all senses, emotions, time. In the experience of those elements you learn and you grow. This is truly the original reason and purpose of human form. You may be looking for a deeper answer. Some decide and require to return into the human form, to return in order to be of assistance.

Yet, as the contract for all souls goes, the entry into human form will require you to start from a blank slate. It will require you to come to a place where the memories of the past or the contract of origin will unfold for you. This requires time, persistence and devotion. For many of you in this space, there is a deeper mission hidden in your very existence.

In this very auspicious time of human history, why are you here?

— *Emmanuel, July 14, 2018, London, UK*

Questioner: Why are we here on Earth and what is our purpose?

Emmanuel: The purpose of life — the question that humankind has been seeking an answer for since the beginning. The human form, in its current existence, is a plane, a space for incubation of human consciousness to experience, to learn and to grow.

Every experience, every life form that is on earth, delivers an important learning for the grand collective of human consciousness. You are part of that. All your actions, all your inactions, every move, thought and experience you have is part of a learning of the collective. The collective grows with all lifetimes that each soul has on this plane.

You have been gifted with this experience. You have been gifted to feel what it feels like to be an individual, to feel what it feels like to have identity, to feel what it feels like to love in separation, to find unity, to find an understanding of individuality and eventually, to find your way back to the collective of human consciousness. You are part of this experiment. The experiment of the growth of human consciousness.

You see, there are two parts that benefit from this experience that you are having. One part is you. The you that is beyond this lifetime, the you that is the soul – and the other part is the collective, the collective that you are a part of, the collective that has sent you here to experience and to learn on behalf of them. This is a gift, even if it may not seem sometimes like a gift in the rollercoaster of all experiences, the spectrum of emotions, the spectrum of challenges. Yet, the truth, the only true purpose of living is life itself. It is the ultimate gift to be part of the growth of human consciousness.

Some individuals will carry a more extended purpose. It will be a purpose that they have particularly agreed upon before entering this current iteration of a lifetime. It may be that they particularly decided to be in service – a service beyond their individual life and experience as individuals. A service that will benefit a community, a society, an entire country or the world itself. This is the power that an individual lifetime can have when directed its purpose. Thank you for your question.

— *Emmanuel, October 31, 2018, Beirut, Lebanon*

Questioner: Do we all have a purpose as individuals, or just some of us? If so, how do we find it?

Emmanuel: Humanity has questioned and asked itself this particular question on an individual basis, as well as as a collective. The answer that we can provide in a simplified manner is: life itself is purpose to exist; experiencing; understanding the depth and the beauty that life itself brings: with relationships, emotions, the detail and the power, the power of love, the power of connection, the power of presence. This in itself carries tremendous purpose. Truly appreciating life in its full details — even the difficult moments; even the difficult emotions — this is the ultimate and the most fundamental basis of purpose of existence on this plane. Beyond, some of you will start to understand that their existence might bring forth a particular mission; a particular desire to assist others in their life, in their evolution; an expression of consciousness through you.

When this internal desire to unfold, to find purpose, arises, the important aspect is to wait patiently; to witness if this desire is driven by emotion, or willpower, or the mind, or a momentary trend. When you witness continuous drive and energy that is insatiable, evolving from your inner being beyond your emotions and beyond your thoughts, this is the fuel for a higher purpose. To see, to feel, and to continuously be open for this drive of higher purpose, one must focus on oneself: alignment, thoughts, emotions, physical wellbeing and inner peace is a requirement to start on assisting more than yourself; assisting others and the collective. You must have a strong foundation.

— *Emmanuel, November 11, 2019, Gulf Region, Middle East*

Questioner: What is the best way to achieve our highest purpose in this life?

Emmanuel: First and foremost, this realization itself is an important opening in anyone's life. The desire to realize the highest purpose in anyone's existence is self-realization in human form: a full understanding of all aspects of reality while alive; discovering the full potential in one's existence beyond all of existence itself; the connection to all of creation.

This journey itself carries tremendous potential to learn and to grow; to continuously be faced with challenges of internal and external kind; truly a lifetime. Many lifetimes can be fulfilled and filled with the desire to self-realize. The side-effect of the journey: the desire to self-realize will provide incredible benefit for your life and for those around you; it will become an inspiration and assistance and it may seem as that is the purpose of your existence. Yet, it is merely a side-effect of your continuous journey.

Never lose sight of the most important element of your existence: the continued evolution to self-realize. And, on this journey, others will be affected positively and you may temporarily take time and embrace these side effects as a purpose. The journey, though, will always call when the time is right to continue; that is when your self-defined purpose must be released.

This is the journey. The journey itself carries purpose. The side effects impact your life and all those around you in the best possible ways. Embrace each of the steps and each of the moments that are [the] result of your awakening process.

— *Emmanuel, November 15, 2019, Gulf Region, Middle East*

Questioner: What is the purpose of human life?

Emmanuel: The grand question: What is the purpose of human existence; what is a single human's purpose and why would one need one? The question can be answered — yet it's a very long answer. To give you the short version: It is a continuation of the expansion of consciousness. Human existence is an extended version of growth and potential for the grand consciousness, the center of all consciousness.

This is an experiment, so to say. You, each of you, are part of the growth of that consciousness. We are the same in that sense.

Everything you experience will eventually get fed into the grand consciousness and it will allow the grand consciousness to evolve and to grow. You all fulfill the grand purpose or underlying purpose, if you so will. Now, to your question: Why would one need to have a purpose anyways if just living life is the purpose. Some souls and some minds seek to have a purpose in order to assist this grand consciousness further in its evolution. You may call it "being in service", in "eternal service", in "grand service" to the grand consciousness. Yet, this is a higher level calling and not many have that calling and need to pursue that calling. Ultimately, if you live your life, you are part of the grand purpose. What we would like to see from our perspective is an evolutionary step in this consciousness field, that we consider as the human consciousness field. So just living your life won't be satisfactory if you want to achieve the next evolutionary step (as humans). We would like to support you in that next evolutionary step.

— *Emmanuel, October 26, 2017, Shanghai, China*

Questioner: What is the highest potential of a human life?

Emmanuel: The human potential is unlimited and very few will reach the higher levels of their potential in the first place. We have witnessed and perceived humanity in all its actions and interactions, through its wars and growth phase, to the days of expansion and today. A single common aspect that we see that always stands in the way of the full potential, is the limitations created by the mind and the heart by the individuals themselves, or their environment. If you can understand that all concepts and realities that you have known are subject to change, you will have a much softer foundation, yet the full spectrum of human potential. It is a practice to continuously step outside of the boxes, frameworks and infrastructures created for you, for your comfort, for your ease. Yet, you will see, outside of those structures of comfort lies tremendous potential. The structures themselves are the aspects that create the limitation in the first place.

— Emmanuel, July 8, 2018, Tuscany, Italy

Questioner: What makes human consciousness different from other developing consciousness?

Emmanuel: In order to truly understand the differences, you would have to understand other forms of consciousness. Many forms of consciousness do not experience material form. The human form was particularly established to experience first and foremost the material forms, to understand duality and separation, to understand all aspects of senses, as well as the experience of time in the material form.

Other forms of consciousness have therein shown interest [in], as well as experienced through the human experience, these elements of material experiences: relations, differences, many aspects of unique form; the experience of connection and love from the eyes of human consciousness, the experience of identity, of creation, the connection to source from the eyes of human consciousness.

All of these elements provide a specific flavor, a specific and unique perspective for human consciousness to be differentiated by other forms of consciousness. They, in their own experience will perceive reality in their own way. Yet truly all of us [are] connected through the one fabric of creation, still individualized in the ways we have experienced and witnessed reality.

— Emmanuel, May 1, 2019, Ibiza, Spain

CHAPTER 10

The Human Experience

You are the bridge between the human plane and the stars. You are the bridge from the human plane to an ascended plane of existence and you shall hold their hands as they walk forward with you, into the light of creation.

— *Raphael, October 29, 2018, Beirut, Lebanon*

Greetings, I am Emmanuel.

Human consciousness evolves through experimentation and expansion. In moments like these, steps are made for human consciousness to evolve. Not every individual is required to be part of this experience, yet through all, the collective experience of human consciousness, they feed the learnings of human consciousness in the way they do.

You are the fabric, you are the content [and] you are the direction. And you are the one that creates the problems and the solutions, all within, for your own growth, for your own sake of evolution, continuously striving for expansion. This is human consciousness, in many ways driven by you, the individual, and the choices made, consciously, and subconsciously.

The attainment of the individual, every single individual in human form, is possible. The self-realization process for every single individual is possible.

The potential within you is and truly unlimited; this is the way we perceive you. Will you start perceiving yourself in the same way?

By being a full potential [being], unlimited in its nature, in human experience and to fully explore the possibilities of the material world, senses, emotions, love and relationship, the elements; aspects, to you, gifted, for consciousness to have this experience. The shift that will happen in the individuals that recognize that every moment in their creation is a gift for their existence, gift to experience as an individual soul, no matter how difficult it may seem in the moment with all its facets. And truly a gift to you and to all of humanity — a gift to all of human consciousness.

You are the conduits; the experience comes to you.

Every moment is the opportunity to seize the limitless potential that is given to you. Every moment therefore carries the limitless potential of your existence. You see, with this perspective, you may potentially change the perspective you have in the moment, the perspective you have on life, the perspective you have on yourself and on existence, potentially assisting you in this reality that you're in, allowing you to navigate this reality with a bit more comfort and direction, allowing for experiences to happen, despite the direct control and the will to avoid these experiences: important learnings to be had for you and the participants of this experience. Every moment allowing this potential, and allowing the choices to be made.

The question: how many of these choices are you aware, and should you be aware of, that are made in every second of your life?

In this path of self-realization, the awareness of the actions is one part to become an observer of the situations; the actions and reactions you may have in their natural and automatic ways, yet still understanding that you are beyond actions and reactions of your being in this immediate moment.

There is an aspect of you, observing, learning, from this very moment. This is an important aspect of human existence and the evolution of consciousness. Conscious observation of the moments of your existence will drive your ability to witness your reality.

Each of these experiences to observe moments of reality will add up to your continued attainment and they will bring you forth on (this/the) self-realization journey combined with the time set aside for quiet contemplation to reset your being into existence.

The human mind operates in a specific way: avoiding immediate discomfort, avoiding threats, [avoiding] pain; yet still seeking experience and interaction within the safety created by the mind, the safety perceived by you, the safety calculated for you, by your subconscious mind, and all the experiences you've had before that directed the creation of those limitations.

Even though well-intended, these creations are aspects that limit human consciousness in its evolution, and only when observed, consciously, will they dissolve, and allow for more freedom; freedom of choice, freedom of energy; the way it is delivered to you in your reality perspective.

That is the freedom you will gain from observing and understanding all the aspects that create the limitations in the first place: to protect you, yet, in exaggerated forms, to limit you, false perceptions of threats, false perceptions of discomfort, the potential outcomes of any outcome of any action limited by the mind, limited by the past, and the projection into the future. You see? The conscious mind in the moment will require [you] to observe which aspects of its reality are formed by past experience or truly a freedom of choice.

This level of attainment and understanding of every single individual will already bring forth a tremendous growth of the collective. This type of reflection requires an impulse, an impulse to stop, and stop the reactive process of the body and the mind, often caused by an accident or sickness, and to bring awareness to the most important thing in your existence: the evolution of your consciousness.

Every moment that you live consciously makes a difference. Every step, every action that is taken consciously makes a difference for the collective. If you understand the power and the strength of your existence to be in the very moment you have, you will have understood the most important aspect of life. This is truly where all your power converges to make this moment reality and to dissolve it in any specific direction, to agree on the direction, and to follow it for the next moment.

When you have understood (that/the) power that lies in each moment of your existence, the power that is given to you to direct it in any certain way, what is the direction that you will take? And, truly, with every step that comes, is it from freedom, freedom from the beliefs and the emotions and past experiences? True freedom of choice will elevate spirit and consciousness.

Other forms of choice will continue an important learning process, yet will not increase the frequency of the entire collective. In order to break that cycle you must understand and observe how you are a participant in that cycle.

This is potentially an important aspect of your life to hear a reality perspective on reality; a direction to consider. In our humble view, we estimate the evolution of consciousness but can never be certain. Truly, human consciousness can [take] directions that are hard to predict or defy aspects of logic.

This is the freedom of consciousness to evolve in any direction it requires to evolve, to truly have the organic growth and space for it to be a fully autonomous system.

You, a part of this human consciousness system.

Thank you for receiving this information and for considering it for your life, the decisions of your life, and the potential outcomes of your future.

— *Emmanuel, August 8, 2019, San Francisco Bay Area, USA*

The Body, Mind, Heart and the Ego

Questioner: How should I find happiness?

Emmanuel: Happiness is not a requirement, and it never was, yet presence is.

How can you be more present as this evolution is happening in your life? And what are the aspects of your life that are keeping you from being present? Your ability to be present in every moment and deeper presence of your full existence will be the key to your fulfillment as this process continues.

— *Emmanuel, March 5, 2018, Budapest, Hungary*

Questioner: What is the role of emotion in humanity's evolution?

Emmanuel: Emotions have been assigned to your function of biology to observe, to experience everything that you're going through — with an extra flavor. This extra flavor allows for the exponential adjustment of your being, for biological feedback of your evolution. So, all your emotions are part of an evolutionary mechanism for your species to continue existing and learning. And in the meantime, you get to have the pleasure to experience what it means to have emotions.

— *Emmanuel, December 31, 2017, San Francisco Bay Area, USA*

Questioner: What is your definition of the human ego?

Emmanuel: The human ego is formulated as a part of your consciousness; as a part of your individualized being. It requires the understanding of self-identification and personalization of this experience. The ego identifies your reality as yours. It perceives relationships as part of its own reality and the continuation of stability of this construct.

The ego perceives itself as "you." Yet, an awakening being will understand that the ego fulfills a specific function: a function that allows for the operations on this plane and for relations to occur. You, as an entire being, are beyond the ego of this current existence. Your conscious awareness will become aware of the ego that has been formulated for you, by you, through your life. It will understand how the ego formulates the desire for control, the desire for recognition, the desire for conditional love.

The part of you that recognizes the ego does not carry desires and wants, it is beyond; still, all part of who you are, understanding that in human form you will always carry this aspect of ego until the very end, understanding that with conscious observation, the patterns of the ego can be learned to be managed appropriately; can be adjusted sustainably; and the ego becomes an ally of your existence: an expression that others can relate to; a reflection of your internal peace and your internal alignment.

— Emmanuel, November 7, 2019, Gulf Region, Middle East

Questioner: What is the wisdom of the body?

Emmanuel: This human form that has been given to you, that you refer to as body, is a complex mechanism beyond the physical perspectives that you may have. Many energetic components, connections, the aspects of your consciousness, are all tied to this physical being. Yet the physical aspects that you perceive are only a small portion of what you consider the body: the physical manifestation for this very plane so that you may experience all aspects of the human form.

The body itself carries intelligence. It carries the intelligence to survive and live on this plane beyond the necessity to think or feel. It will provide the basics, yet the most important aspects to keep you alive on this very plane. This in itself: the ability to understand, to live within an environment in balance and always adjusting to the circumstances, is the wisdom of the body.

It recognizes beyond your mind, it feels beyond your heart, its ability to sense threats, its ability to sense beauty and warmth are beyond your ability to comprehend, yet always available to you. This will require listening to the body itself.

In environments of modern life, many humans have forgotten to listen to the intelligence and the wisdom available through the body. It is lost in the distractions of daily life, in the important work and aspects of life. Aspects of relationship, aspects of emotions and always deprioritizing the wisdom.

The intelligence of the body is beyond its goal to keep you alive. It is deeper. It is tied to aspects of your connection to this planet, to your connection with your surroundings, to your connection to food and water, to your connection to the sun, to the wind, to [all] the elements that are available to you. You see, sheer endless wisdom available and experience-able through the body. Will you take the time and the moment to listen?

— *Emmanuel, June 14, 2019, Gulf Region, Middle East*

Questioner: What is the purpose of the human mind?

Emmanuel: In a unified collective mind, in a connection beyond your identity and personality, and the connection that provides you with your essence, the energy of the universe, the energy of this planet, you continuously are provided for. All questions become irrelevant in this form of awareness; connection.

Yet, the human mind demands; the human mind operates and makes sure you are alive. It requires personality. It requires duality. It requires questions to be answered, to evaluate safety, to evaluate decisions, and actions. You will start to receive many of these answers to your questions in your silent moments. You will start to see that some questions may not require any answer at the moment, and the deeper level of trust and surrender sometimes provides all the answers that you require.

— *Emmanuel, November 2, 2019, Gulf Region, Middle East*

Finding Inner Guidance

Questioner: In the human form, we are often disconnected from source energy and we live in a different density. Faced with this difficult situation, how can we seek guidance, how can we improve our intuition and find our inner voice and guidance?

Emmanuel: The human form, in all its material aspects, is overwhelming. The body, the mind and the heart are loud voices, and they require attention at any given point. Each of them will try to take control.

The key is to take care of all parts of your being in this form: The body requires attention, the heart desires to be held, and the mind requires to be appreciated for the work it does. When you take care of all aspects of your being, you can start to find quiet and silence of those aspects.

Only upon finding this silence will you start seeing the deep connection that you have already to a higher consciousness, yet it will require first these steps: taking care of the body, the mind and the heart; and truly seeking quiet, so that you can hear the voice of creation.

— *Emmanuel, April 5, 2018, Gulf Region, Middle East*

Questioner: How do I learn to distinguish the voice of spirit from the voice of my ego? How do I learn to follow my inner voice?

Emmanuel: The voice of the ego will often come with conditions; will often come with judgments and opinions. It will often have aspects of limitation and belief.

The true voice of the soul, of higher consciousness, has a different "weight." It will come unconditionally; pure. And, you will feel the truth of that voice in every aspect of your being. Your mind or your heart may not like what you receive — yet you will know it is the truth. It will have a resonance, a weight, that you cannot deny. That is the difference between the voice of the ego and the voice of your soul.

— *Emmanuel, April 5, 2018, Gulf Region, Middle East*

Questioner: How can you know if it is your mind or your heart talking to you?

Emmanuel: The mind and the heart have both their own agenda. Either way, we believe that both the heart and the mind are constructs that are important to your existence: the mind to protect you from experiences that you've had, to make sense of your environment, to make sure that you survive; the heart, in a way allowing you to experience your environment in its full extent, all emotions guiding you, directing you in a certain way, often towards comfort, sometimes towards experience.

Either way, there is a different state of presence, a state of presence that is beyond the mind and the heart, that is beyond thoughts and emotions; a state of presence that is connected to higher dimensions of consciousness. In this moment of quiet, your perception will open: your perception to higher realms as well as your perception in human form. Appreciating the mind, appreciating the heart for their service to you, yet understanding that there is a form of presence that carries an even more important aspect of your being is the key.

— *Emmanuel, October 11, 2018, Gulf Region, Middle East*

Questioner: As humans, we are required to make decisions every day, and we are guided to listen to our heart. How do we hear the heart more clearly?

Emmanuel: All aspects of your being can be influencing factors for your decisions; the body, the mind, the heart, and the spirit. All aspects of your being have equal say. The current understanding of your society is that the mind shall carry the most weight and decisions and it shall make decisions in a way to protect you, protect those around you and to optimize your life in a certain way that is acceptable to the rest.

The heart and the body have been suppressed, the spirit has not been listened to.

When you open yourself up to other forms of influence for your decisions you may hear the heart, or you may hear your body. Maybe you may hear your spirit guiding you, beyond your mind.

You will require to practice and understand how the mind operates and how it will settle. Your mind is different from the mind of others; it has been conditioned in different ways, by different experiences. It has been given much power, yet it operates from wounds of the past. A whole understanding and appreciation of your mind will allow you to hear more [of] what your heart has to say and beyond that you may even settle the aspects of your heart.

Since the heart can also make decisions based on wounds of the past, spirit, your higher self, will guide you in a way that is beyond the mind and the heart — and it may allow you to see milestones that are far more important to you than the ones that you can see or feel.

— *Emmanuel, October 14, 2018, Gulf Region, Middle East*

Questioner: How does intuition work and how do we best use it?

Emmanuel: Intuition is a function of a human being. It is an aspect of your higher consciousness to provide you with information that goes beyond the mind and the heart. Aspects of your body may as well influence this source of information. The higher self, the higher consciousness of your being, is tied and connected to aspects of your soul, as well as to divine sources. Often, intuition will provide perspectives from these higher planes. This may be contradictory to the aspects of your logic, it may be contradictory to the aspects of your heart, it may even feel unsafe to your body, yet there is a reason for this information source to be available to you.

When all aspects of your mind, your heart, and your body have not provided you the information that you require to hear, this is a source that you can rely on.

Yet, it will require practice: Practice quieting the mind in its sheer dominance of your life. Practice in quieting the heart and all the emotions that want to be heard and have not, and practice to listen beyond the aspects, beyond the body, the desires of comfort and rest.

A deeper knowing that is available to you, yet requires work on your end to find your center and balance and to allow this voice to rise within you.

— Emmanuel, June 14, 2019, Gulf Region, Middle East

Shaping Reality

Questioner: What's the meaning of manifestation?

Emmanuel: Manifestation is the understanding and alignment that all aspects of your being are connected to your material environment. In simpler words, when your mind, your heart, and your soul are in alignment, then every experience that is coming into being is coming from this alignment, it is coming from a conscious presence.

Some experiences come without that awareness; it may seem random, [it] may seem like you are the victim, or the subject of an experience — yet there is always an aspect that you are connected to that assists, and the manifestation of this experience is often connected to a deeper learning.

When there is a level of learning that is ready to come to completion, the alignment of your mind and your heart and soul will allow for the manifestation of aspects of your desires and wants. This is, yet, though, a rather rare opportunity, and most just can dream of this state of immediate manifestation. Some of you progressing in your awakening process will see manifestation and synchronicities much more often than others; most of it is due to your more heightened awareness and some of it is due to the clarity of your karmic record.

— *Emmanuel, October 11, 2018, Gulf Region, Middle East*

CHAPTER 11

Facing Difficult Emotions & Challenges

You have chosen to be in this world, in this incarnation, in this environment with these choices and the request for learning. You have been challenged and provided with the circumstances to learn, the opportunities to understand and grow. Yet some of these opportunities and circumstances to grow are perceived as negative by the mind and by the heart. They are perceived as uncomfortable. They are perceived as unwanted.

The moment you change your perspective, you will start to see that everything on this plane serves you and truly you. All moments, all circumstances, all challenges, are truly in service to you and your growth. Once you embody this truth, you will see that the obstacles will become your best friend.

— Emmanuel, January 26, 2019, Gulf Region, Middle East

Greetings, I'm Emmanuel.

The time has come for you to face all that requires to be faced: all elements of your being that have been suppressed unprocessed; hidden from yourself; hidden from others. The time has come to observe the process, to digest, and let go of these parts of you.

This process sometimes will require overcoming your own attachment to comfort. Even facing these elements of your being might be emotional. And, with the right distance and the right perspective, all facets of your being can be observed without impacting you in the moment. This is your ability to observe and to process what requires to be processed.

Some of you will be required to process more elements: of your environment, elements of your family, ancestry and lineage. Some of you will process societal concepts, societal fears, and suppressed trauma. Each of you have the ability to convert experiences of any size into wisdom and realization. Yet, this process must happen within a living human being. Some processes happen on an unconscious or subconscious level. Some processes happen in dream phases or in altered states.

You are making progress as these elements are processing through you, even if it may seem that you are unable to produce and to create according to the values of society. This gift and this ability to process experiences into realizations is the highest service to humankind.

Yet, first, you must observe all the elements within you that require attention; and, the work that we have performed today might bring some of these elements to the surface. You will always have the option to suppress again, or to move it to a future time, or to rationalize it away; to deprioritize other elements of your life ahead of this. You are the owner of your life and we are just bringing reminders and assistance along.

The pathway to empowerment requires facing all the elements that are unprocessed, as this will free up energy and flow within your system:

thoughts and emotions will be more expressive and expansive; a new vitality will come to you as the energy utilized and locked to manage unprocessed experiences will be freed.

Your most natural state; your true self in human form; your full potential in human form; this is our goal for you. You may choose many different ways to address parts of you that require attention. The simplest way is to observe from all perspectives possible; without judgment, without emotion: pure observation and witnessing, allowing this occurrence of the past to become a realization for the collective. The collective will not store emotions; it will only store realizations for its growth and evolution.

We are grateful for you to be open to receive and to be walking this path in your life; to be called into a higher truth within you; to allow this opening within you to expand; to be fueled and assisted.

— Emmanuel, November 15, 2019, Gulf Region, Middle East

Greetings, I'm Raphael.

Every step of the way is preparation for the next step: no step is ever backwards; no time is ever wasted. Remember, even experiences that are seemingly irrelevant, that are seemingly complicated and unnecessary, carry the infinite potential of learning and growth. Your ability to receive and to observe and to be present is the only obstacle to make each moment truly full of benefits for you and all involved.

The goals and expectations set by your own mind; by society for you by those that were your guardians before. You are the only one to live your life: the boundaries set, the expectations set, create a certain framework for you to operate within. Understanding the importance of certain frames for societal functionalities, for the survival and the benefit of others, and observing automatic behaviors of yours: patterns of thinking and patterns of feeling.

It is time for you to extend beyond the frames created by yourself and by the outside. It is time to feel the potential and power that lies within you; the expression of creation, the full potential considered.

Thank you for receiving this work. It is our effort to support you on this pathway forward.

— Raphael, November 15, 2019, Gulf Region, Middle East

Our work is to support you; to empower you to become the highest potential individual that you can be in this lifetime. Thank you for receiving this work.

The unfolding of the adjustments will be manifold: mental and emotional ease with life itself, with relationships; the most important: your relationship with yourself. Understanding, appreciating, and loving the being that you are — all parts of it — even those parts that are hard to love, hard to forgive, hard to forget: those parts of you require even more acceptance, compassion and love, from no one else but you.

The shackles that you have are the ones that you're holding onto; the limitations are the ones that you believe; you are truly powerful individuals; powerful beings in human form.

Thank you for listening to my words.

— Raphael, November 11, 2019, Gulf Region, Middle East

Fear

Questioner: Why do we have fear inside?

Emmanuel: Thank you for your question. Fear is another aspect of the mind to keep you safe. It is an aspect that has created boundaries and limitations so that you can stay alive. Most fear is based on experience and the experience of those that have raised you and the experience you may have gained in previous incarnations.

These experiences have formed belief systems about your reality and so these belief systems created a structure for you to operate in. This structure is for your safety and it is for you to understand that it is merely a structure. A structure to be overcome. A structure that is not real in the first place. A structure that is an illusion. All fears shall fall apart in the face of trust and surrender.

You shall see, the universe and all of creation has always been taking care of you, beyond the fears that you have believed to have kept you safe. Fear has offered you learning and opportunity to grow, to come to these conclusions by yourself. Here we are.

While I am delivering you this conclusion, will you receive it deeply and will you apply this conclusion to your life? Or will you wait until you come to the conclusion yourself?

— *Emmanuel, October 31, 2018, Beirut, Lebanon*

Questioner: Where does fear come from?

Emmanuel: Fear is an aspect of your subconscious mind. It is a protective measure for survival and understanding that through fear, natural and environmental threats are understood, completed, categorized and serving your continuous life. These functions do not always operate as planned and fear can be nourished by aspects of your mind: by trauma, by experiences, by perceived threats; by stories of perceived threats. Truly, there is no limitation for the subconscious mind to create many aspects to fuel fear.

Ultimately, all aspects of your subconscious mind are aspects of your growth, providing you with the opportunity to see beyond the fear itself, to see beyond the aspects of perceived reality. Fear becomes a friend. Fear becomes an ally to provide the opportunity to evolve as an individual and as a collective.

— *Emmanuel, April 18, 2019, San Francisco Bay Area, USA*

Questioner: How do I work with the fear I feel inside?

Emmanuel: Fear is your friend. It shows you in many ways the parts of you that you have been rejecting. All emotions have a purpose. The human form is complete and therefore perfect by design. When you have understood the lesson that fear is trying to teach you, it will let go. Channeling the fear into another activity or emotion may give you immediate comfort, yet will not solve the ultimate challenge. The deep learning is understanding the origin of the fear. And facing it with gratitude for the lesson that it brings into your life. Only then, the cycle will be complete. I hope this makes sense to you. It will in time.

— *Emmanuel, March 5, 2018, Budapest, Hungary*

Questioner: How can we deepen our trust in the universe?

Emmanuel: The trust has always been there along the way — it has been broken. When a baby is born, it has no concept of trusting, or consciously making a decision, or evaluating its environment. It just "is," and it fully surrenders to the existence of its environment. This is the original form of trust that you're all given with.

Over time, this trust is broken and adjusted. Experiences of external input, of making sense and meaning of the external reality, provide for a picture of the world that is less trustworthy; education, relationships, yet also various experiences of your own; various dangers, evaluations of safety.

Ultimately, the goal will become to overcome all thoughts, all conditioning, and to return to this original trust that you're all given with. It is the many layers that have been built on top of this original trust that constrict your perspective, layer by layer. You must remove all that covers this original trust — original trust in all of existence.

Layer by layer, you must observe in which moments you don't trust, in which ways you don't trust your environment or yourself, and as you observe these ways of being, allow yourself to surrender slightly more. And, to let go of this conditioning, allow yourself to step a bit further into the unknown. Despite your concerns, doubts and fears, move yourself outside of the comfort that has built over time to restrict you.

You are unlimited beings living limited lives. You can find unlimited trust in every moment again, yet it will require practice and continuous contemplation.

— *Emmanuel, November 29, 2019, Vienna, Austria*

Feeling Lost

Questioner: I don't feel clarity in my life around what I should be focused on, I feel scattered and I am looking for guidance.

Emmanuel: In general, all options are equally important in human existence, they are all part of the collective growth of human consciousness. Their value is important, no matter what you think is important or worthwhile pursuing.

It is the judgement and the fear of the unknown, as this path has not unfolded for you and is a natural aspect of existence. Doubt and fear about a specific path, and many options for you to pursue; to learn and to grow.

So, where is the limiting factor that stops you from moving forward? It is expectation: the expectation of a specific outcome on this path that you want to follow. It may be your expectation, or the expectation that you believe others will have for you, or the expectation of your parents for yourselves that you carry with you. Expectation will ultimately stop you from pursuing a specific path.

Now that you are aware, you have methods to look into how to manage your expectations for a future that has not unfolded yet: Can you be easier with yourself? Can you allow yourself to walk a path of mistakes and many learnings, even though they may not obviously result in the success your environment has defined for you?

Can you walk this path in the face of knowing there will be mistakes, and there will be challenges, and there will be pain; yet every morning you will make steps forward in your desire to learn, in your curiosity to grow, in your desire to be of service to yourself but also to those around you? This is my perspective for you.

— *Emmanuel, July 14, 2018, London, UK*

Questioner: If you're lost in a journey that you're taking, how do you know what is the right next step to take?

Emmanuel: All journeys lead to the same destination. There are different routes, full of different experiences and learnings, some of which you might judge as "difficult," or "lost." Yet, in the end, they all provide important learning and growth.

Without judgement and opinion, all experiences of your life have served you to become who you are, and have provided you the full spectrum of experiences: from love and joy, to sadness and anger. One would not exist without the other, you see?

One cannot be "found," without being "lost."

The spectrum of experiences helps you understand what the right balance is, and understand what choices are. Aside from the journey, the aspect that will change everything for you is your ability to be present in every moment; to truly understand all aspects of the moment; all aspects of your being in relationship to the moment.

This very moment is the one where all your power comes together. All decisions are made right now. Your ability to understand and to become more present will influence all decisions in your life, and all of the journeys to come.

— *Emmanuel, September 15, 2019, San Francisco Bay Area, USA*

Questioner: It's almost as if I feel lost as a human, even homesick for some other place; how do I learn to feel at home here?

Emmanuel: Not all that have received the gift of human form will feel comfort. Some of you feel distant from this experience; foreign to this experience; alien within the human form; distant from the material experience.

Yet here you are. A part of you has chosen to be here in this very form for your, as well as for others' benefit. All life, all experiences of a soul in human form, play an important role. Yours still remains to unfold, yet it will, and you will find the purpose that you are seeking.

You will find the support that you require to assist you through the difficulties of the human experience, to provide you the opening to higher levels of consciousness. And, through these openings, you will start to remember the true purpose and the true reason for your current lifetime. Allow patience to be part of your life. Allow love for the uncertain to be part of your life and remain open to receive.

— Emmanuel, May 26, 2019, Budapest, Hungary

Questioner: What lessons am I to learn from feeling so lost?

Emmanuel: The human mind and the human heart have overwhelming ability to completely take over your perception of reality. It is by design, so you can be fully present in your experience — no matter how difficult or beautiful it would be.

Yet, in this time of special circumstance, we recommend you listen to a higher voice within you: A part of your being that is beyond your heart and beyond your mind. A part of you that is beyond your identity of this lifetime. A part of you that has existed for a very long time. You have access to this part of you. It is you. It is the only true you.

For you to have a clear connection with this part of you, you will require to quiet your heart and your mind and to take care of your body in the best possible way; only this way can you be present to the voice of your true self.

— Emmanuel, April 3, 2018, Gulf Region, Middle East

Questioner: How can I be of service to others when I feel I am lost?

Emmanuel: Do not identify yourself with the wounds that you carry. You are more than the experiences that you had in this lifetime. If your identity carries these emotions and the aspects of your past, you will never find freedom to the extent that you can be of service to others. You are not your wounds, do you understand?

Questioner: Honestly, no, because these wounds are part of what have shaped me into who I am today, and they still live inside of me. I am not sure what you mean when you say I should "not identify myself" with them — I don't even know what that means, nor how to achieve it.

Emmanuel: You will understand when the time comes that you are not your experience; that your experience is in service to your growth and to the realization that you are beyond this human experience. If the experience still is close to your identity, there is more work to be done.

We encourage you to look deeper, finding ways to distance yourself from the experience. Remember, the experience is your friend: it has been in service to you, not the other way around.

— *Emmanuel, April 11, 2018, Gulf Region, Middle East*

Pain and Suffering

Questioner: Why is there so much suffering in the world, and why are good people not protected from harm?

Emmanuel: Challenges, difficulties and hardship are part of the spectrum of human experience; one does not exist without the other. Continuation of being challenged is an element of nature and of consciousness to understand how to grow, how to mature. Suffering, on the other hand, is a mechanism of the human mind to attach to the pain and the difficulties that are [ahead]. This attachment continues even after the pain itself has gone. This is what we; what you; consider as suffering.

Pain and difficulties are opportunities to learn — always will be — until the very end of existence. All moments that are considered challenging; difficult; are always an opportunity to grow. With this understanding, you will see, as you surrender to receive the potential realizations in the moment, your reality will start to shift as well.

Good people, bad people; based on whose judgment? Values are defined by you; defined by societies; defined by humanity. Deep inside of you is the ultimate value system. Individuals that continually assist other humans and perform good deeds are not exempt from hardship or challenges in life. In fact, some of them seek even bigger challenges to grow even faster: it is part of the fuel that makes them who they are. Some of them have understood that the challenge itself is a continuous opportunity and trigger to learn, and to grow, and to apply even more the gifts that are given to them.

— Emmanuel, November 11, 2019, Gulf Region, Middle East

Questioner: Do you sense any great pain coming to humanity soon?

Emmanuel: Yes. Pain will always be part of this plane. It is part of your experience. It is the trigger to move; to actively operate, face challenges and difficulties. And, this wave of pain that will enter your plane will serve as your final test to growth and evolution in consciousness.

We do not perceive this pain to be negative, yet in human form that is easier said than done. Your ability to transcend this judgment of pain and perceive all aspects of your reality as an opportunity to grow, as a challenge that can be faced alone or together, will be your key on this path. And, you will receive assistance along this path from us, and others like us.

— Emmanuel, December 12, 2018, San Francisco Bay Area, USA

Anger, Guilt, and Shame

Questioner: What is the purpose of shame and guilt?

Emmanuel: Shame and guilt are somehow the most misunderstood teachers of humanity and the human form. They both carry important lessons yet the lessons cannot be retrieved until new perspectives are seen.

Shame, as a teacher, is based on your understanding of duality; your understanding that an experience is positive or negative by your judgement, or your judgement of others. The perspective that we will recommend to you, and all of humanity, is the perspective of non-duality: a distant view on the experience rather than an emotional view on the experience itself.

Perceiving experience and all human interactions as divine, no matter how difficult those were, will assist you to have an additional perspective, and if you are able to integrate this perspective, you will see that the emotions of shame and guilt will start to loosen their grip on you; important teachers; new perspective and understanding non-duality.

— *Emmanuel, July 8, 2018, Tuscany, Italy*

Questioner: What is the role of shame in the development in our culture, and how can large groups of people complete this emotional experience?

Emmanuel: Similar to all experiences that are available in the human body, emotions carry an instrumental aspect of it. Shame is an emotion that is triggered by the emotions and the expectations of the environment.

Emotions, if not completed, are stored, like memories, until they are fully expressed and completed as a learning opportunity for you. The current situation of all of humankind: unlimited sources of emotions unexpressed — including shame and guilt, anger and sadness — waiting to be completed, waiting to be seen, uncovered, understood, and listened to.

The only way is for the individual to first make the effort to look inside; to bring the courage to let these aspects that have been limiting come to the surface, to find the right environments with other individuals or alone to complete the expression — the understanding of the emotion itself.

Incomplete learnings will continue in the next generation; it always has been, it always will be. Some of your learnings will include the completions of many generations before you. You are the current version of all of these incomplete lessons.

You are the one to complete and end cycles. This is a responsibility you must understand and willingly take on, and you will find freedom for yourself and all the generations before you, all the generations that will come after you, as a collective gift from you. Thank you for your question.

— Emmanuel, October 20, 2019, San Francisco Bay Area, USA

Questioner: What can we learn from our emotions, and, especially, what is the purpose of anger?

Emmanuel: All human emotions are built and designed to give you the balance and spectrum of the human experience. They allow you to see in different colors and perspectives. They allow you to perceive your environment and yourself from so many different angles. This experience of emotion will give you the space to learn and to grow.

For the growth to happen, the emotion needs to be completed in its expression. Only then [the] realization of the mind can happen, and, beyond the realization of the mind, the realization of the soul will then eventually complete the circle of understanding.

Once this cycle is complete, new learning and experience may arise for you, and similarly, you will go through the motions of human experience until this learning is complete as well. Anger is just another aspect of this learning process: an aspect of emotion; a color to add to the spectrum of human experience.

— Emmanuel, November 11, 2018, Gulf Region, Middle East

Grief and Trauma

Questioner: What is grief?

Emmanuel: Grief is an aspect of the human emotional system to allow you to deal with major upset, sadness, anger, loss. Grief is a timeframe in which the mind and the heart and the body can process this upset. It is a natural construct for you to be able to move on. Grief is important for cultures to move through major upset and trauma. If this timeframe is suppressed or foregone, it will ultimately carry the scars into the future. Incomplete healing will always show itself in different ways, especially in future generations. Incomplete healing may turn into suffering and a continued pain that never ends. Grief is welcome and should be perceived as a positive force.

— *Emmanuel, October 14, 2018, Gulf Region, Middle East*

Questioner: What is the role of childhood trauma and emotional wounds in evolution and is it necessary or relevant to heal them?

Emmanuel: Thank you for your question. All aspects of human experience are designed to be part of a learning experience to assist humanity to grow. Human consciousness learns from all the individual learnings; all individual experiences fuel the human consciousness field. All resolutions and realizations equally fuel this human consciousness field. Your resolution will make a difference. Yet, if you will not resolve, other parts of consciousness will start to resolve a similar experience, so that ultimately human consciousness can grow from this one learning.

You see, all your lives, all your experiences — all facets and moments — are microscopic experiments for consciousness to learn and to grow, continuously experiencing life through you.

The answer to your question is: "yes, it is relevant," and, "no, it is not relevant." You may still choose to disregard the experiences as irrelevant and move on, yet you will see there will be a stronger peace within if you find the strength and the courage to uncover the necessary peace and resolution.

— Emmanuel, April 12, 2019, San Francisco Bay Area, USA

Questioner: How can my inner child heal and if I don't have any recollection of what happened to me as a child?

Emmanuel: Healing happens on many different levels, some of which are not conscious to you. If you seek to do healing on a conscious level, you're first required to bring all aspects of your subconscious to the forefront of your awareness. Humanity has developed many methods to reach aspects of the subconscious, to retrieve those aspects that are in the dark.

Once you have awareness, you can address these elements one-by-one and you may see that some memories or thoughts will carry strong emotions. And, strong emotions of the past will establish a certain belief and perspective on your environment. This perspective will frame your world and reality.

In our work, we want you to be free of any of those frames. We want you to see the universe in a much wider perspective; beyond the individual identity you carry, beyond your personal experience and wounds, beyond the learnings you have made as the human that you are in this very individual form. This is true realization; this is the path to self-realization. Healing your inner child is one step in that direction.

— Emmanuel, October 14, 2018, Gulf Region, Middle East

Questioner: Why do some people experience great human suffering, like war or famine?

Emmanuel: Suffering, from the perspective of non-material existence, does not carry the same weight as it does in human experience;

therefore, many of these experiences are truly chosen. They are truly a part of the growth of the individual soul that has chosen to be part of this experience, individually or as a collective.

During this experience, learnings will arise, and opportunities for the collective to learn in unison with other souls. War and famine are perfect examples for important action within human existence, within the human collective. Learnings of collaboration, union; learnings of alignment and maturity — beyond [one's] own identity — have not arrived. These learnings will eventually provide the fertile ground to find peace within and to find peace in the human collective; to understand that this plane is truly reserved and provided for all: the pleasures, the beauties, the sufferings and the emotions, the pain and the difficulties are equally [important] elements of this human experience. The sacrifice of choice, to provide an important mirror for all those around, is and always will be a true selection of brave decisions by individual souls.

You are not much different than those that are suffering; those that are suffering are not much different than you are. The equal opportunity to learn, the equal opportunity to serve as a vessel of learning and growth is part of your lives and you may indeed choose grave pain and suffering for a future life to be in service for yourself and for those around you for the human consciousness to grow and collect the necessary knowledge and experiences.

— *Emmanuel, April 23, 2019, Gulf Region, Middle East*

Conflict and Forgiveness

Greetings, I am Michael.

The reason for my appearance is the continuous and ongoing battles in all of you. The battles inside are often the reasons for the battles outside; a continuous and conscious understanding of your inner world. The parts of you that are in conflict — some parts of you unconscious or subconscious — it is your responsibility to attend to this conflict; to observe the conflict from both sides; to understand both positions in relation to survival and growth; safety.

Some of these perspectives of the inner conflict will be illusionary fears that might never occur; probabilities of potential outcomes so low yet so strongly in your being, directing a specific pathway for you. These positions, the root of all these positions in conflict, must be understood, must be reflected upon; and a higher conscious version of you becomes the judge to choose a specific path, despite the opinions within yourself. You will always be given choices and reasons for each path; rational or emotional reasons to choose.

In deep reflection, it can only be a higher-conscious version of you that chooses to receive the highest probable outcome for you. Important lessons to complete; and for some of you, even more important missions to exist in this current lifetime, to operate in a way that is beyond the collection of experience, to become a vessel of the divine and to assist humanity in its evolution and its growth.

This path cannot be taken until the deepest and the strongest fears inside have been addressed. The deepest conflicts inside of you will continue, even throughout your service. Before choosing any pathway specific to service, you must understand yourself in the deepest possible ways and resolve any potential conflicts. Establish ways to resolve future conflicts in the highest and purest form. Fears, doubts, worries, existential crises will never cease to exist, yet the way you react, receive and adjust to the circumstances will change.

Thank you for listening to my words.

— *Michael, November 15, 2019, Gulf Region, Middle East*

Questioner: How can we foster the development of peace and love here in Syria?

Emmanuel: Thank you for your question. It is a selfless act to think beyond the borders of your own being, of your own identity. You are the maker of your surroundings, of your roots, and of the region that has housed you and many generations before you. You are the land, you are the earth, you are this society.

The peace inside of you will carry peace outside of you. You are intrinsically connected to all beings around. The effect of the outside has always been humanity's challenge and also its biggest test. Can you, despite the difficulties and the challenges outside, remain [with] the light from within? Can you, despite loss and grieving, carry love and an open heart with you? Can you continue to love yourself, despite shame and guilt? These questions are for you to answer. This is also the key for peace overall and not all humans will succeed in understanding this concept.

They will always carry a perspective of victimhood to the circumstances around them and it may be easier said than done. Yet this is your ultimate challenge — to continue the peace within; to affect the peace without.

Your own individual growth, healing, and peace inside is the most leveraged way to bring peace without — and additionally, you may wish to include others in your practice to find this peace within.

You may continue to connect with other beings of light to continuously foster this momentum and vibration. You may continuously fuel this connection with others of light to support the communities that require this light.

You will see that one and one is not two — light multiplies in a different way. You will see that the growth will be exponential, [as] more [individuals that] come together in peaceful ways, in connection to a deeper understanding of themselves, [and] a deeper understanding of the divine. We are supporting your effort as individuals and as groups of beings that have been faced with difficult challenges in the past.

When you open your hearts in deep contemplation, alone or together, at sites that carry sacred energy, you may even have a direct connection to some divine forces like ourselves and we may come to assist in certain situations. This is an opportunity, yet not a guarantee. You will always carry the highest power in your own life. Thank you for your question.

— Emmanuel, November 2, 2018, Damascus, Syria

Questioner: How do we know when conflict has served its purpose and it is time to move on?

Emmanuel: There is no general answer to your question. Conflict: the opposition of two standing points; two perspectives. The understanding that there are two equal and valid perspectives, in a non-dual world, equally important and valuable. There is no requirement to continue any conflict once it is understood that all perspectives fuel the entirety. New perspectives are always welcome as they bring a new facet of understanding, a new facet to realize; to deepen the existing understanding.

Conflict is the resistance to changing perspectives and allowing other perspectives to be included in one's [own perspective]. One is not right over the other, and if you refer to the conflict inside, it is the same perspective that will give you peace: that both standpoints always should be considered equal, no matter the judgment, no matter the belief or the circumstances. Allowing the full expression of these standpoints will complete the realization of this conflict.

— Emmanuel, November 15, 2019, Gulf Region, Middle East

Questioner: How do we truly forgive people? Is it a conscious effort, or does it happen naturally over time?

Emmanuel: Thank you for your question. Forgiveness, as an act itself, allows [you] to understand a present moment of conflict, of violation, of difficulty to forgive the other or yourself; [it] is an opening to a deeper healing, a release from the attachment to that past moment. This is how the journey starts; yet not how it ends.

Forgiveness is the opening that will be created within your heart to understand that there are different perspectives; realities in which some will have hardship to grow and to learn, even beyond their will and their desire. This is the grand interplay that is existent on this plane of humanity. Compassion for yourself and for others, despite difficult to understand experiences; expanding your heart even more to hold all of those — even the ones that you perceive are not worthy of your love — they are the ones that require it the most; and forgiveness will be transformed into unconditional understanding and unconditional love.

In this space, there is no victim or villain, and no one to forgive; no one to be excused. There is only love. This space is beyond your mind. This space is beyond your value systems and your emotions. You have this space within you, and it will require practice to continuously unfold and connect with this particular space of unconditional love.

— *Emmanuel, November 11, 2019, Gulf Region, Middle East*

Questioner: How can we heal the pattern of victimhood and powerlessness?

Emmanuel: Patterns of "victim," "villain" — or even "hero" itself — are all aspects of an interplay until they are completed. The completion can be initiated by each party. The purpose of this interplay is to receive the true understanding of the perspectives of all of the participants; a deep knowing, and an understanding of the importance for one's growth to have had this experience in the first place, for the growth of the collective.

Once peace has been found within each party, then the cycle will be complete, and the role designated will no longer continue to have the same hold that it did before, yet each party understands the importance of having played their role for their own learning and growth.

All humans have been victims before — and villains — and saviors; in this lifetime, and in many lifetimes before. All of these cycles are for the purpose of learning and growth. Understand the power that you have to complete this cycle.

— Emmanuel, September 15, 2019, San Francisco Bay Area, USA

CHAPTER 12

Love, Relationships, Sexual Energy, Masculine & Feminine

Relationships are a fundamental aspect of the human experience: your relationship to yourself, to others and your environment. As you move into the realization that you are not separate — that you never have been, that your consciousness is continuously and has always been connected to each other — your perception of your relationships will change: your relationship with yourself, your understanding [of] who you are in the grand scheme of the cosmos, but, also, your relationship to others in understanding how you are connected beyond this human form, and your relationship to all consciousness beyond the human consciousness.

— Emmanuel, March 18, 2018, Bali, Indonesia

Love

Questioner: What is love?

Emmanuel: Love is a big question. The way we perceive love in its many forms, the way it is experienced in human form and the way it exists continuously in the universe ... Love is the very fabric of existence.

It is unconditional, multi-dimensional, and always present; the very fabric of existence, an unconditional thread of light and energy. You are part of this unconditional fabric, you and all of the planets and the stars and the universes. This is what we refer to as the "unconditional love of creation."

Love, as a concept in human interaction, has a different meaning from our perspective; often an aspect of conditional connection, a deep connection, an energetic bond, yet rarely will it develop to an unconditional level. A teacher and a test of challenge and growth, ultimately the bridge to the one true unconditional love: the unconditional love of creation.

If you can perceive human love as your teacher and your stepping stone for a bigger understanding of [the] unconditional love of creation, you will understand our perspective of all love. Thank you for your question.

— *Emmanuel, July 8, 2018, Tuscany, Italy*

Questioner: Are there different forms of love?

Emmanuel: Love is perceived in many ways in the human form: the love of relationship, the love of existence, the love of connection. All love is a deep experience of growth, yet, on a lower level it is conditional: it is connected to direct experience; it is connected to Karma, it is connected to learning.

Beyond this level of love there is what we perceive as unconditional love: the true love of creation, the love that permeates through all living and not-living existence in the universe, the love that does not know any boundaries, the love that is available to all, all the time. The perception of this type of love will require higher states of consciousness.

You see, love comes in many forms, and it serves tremendous purpose, and it is a guiding path to the highest form of love, which is the unconditional love of creation.

— *Emmanuel, March 18, 2018, Bali, Indonesia*

Questioner: Why is human nature always longing for love, and once love is found, why does it create such a turbulent emotional experience?

Emmanuel: The connection that is intrinsic within you; the connection to existence itself, the fabric that ties all planes to each other, is what we consider the "love of creation:" a form of unconditional love and energy that provides; that exists through all planes and through all existence. The attraction to be "one" again — as this human experience is a momentary separation to experience individuality. Yet, truly, your inner nature knows the connection of all existence, and the glue itself is love, experiencing and exploring different forms of connection and different forms of love; with conditions, with complications, with challenges; the desire to unite in conflict with the desire to stay unique and separate.

The turbulence is part of the growth process and the learning itself. Every interaction assists the human collective to grow. Every experience is information that provides perspective and potential to learn. This is the reason for experiencing this plane in human form: for understanding and learning, and that love is a connected force that unites all of existence and in this case, it becomes the fuel for learning and growth on this plane.

— *Emmanuel, November 15, 2019, Gulf Region, Middle East*

Questioner: What should we know about romantic love?

Emmanuel: To fully surrender. That is all you need to know. Thank you for your question.

— *Emmanuel, April 12, 2019, San Francisco Bay Area, USA*

Questioner: How do you define unconditional love?

Emmanuel: Unconditional love is the energy and the force that binds all of existence together. All planes, material and non-material; all existence, consciously and unconsciously alive; is bound through this fabric: the unconditional love of creation and energy that is limitless, yet does not carry any specific source. This energy continuously provides for all planes, including yours. It is the energy upon which all your lives are based on — all life on this planet is based on. This continuous flow of energetic consciousness is what we consider unconditional love.

It is the perfect representation of a non-judging existence: unaware of its own existence, yet continuously providing; without categorization, limitation, or judgment, in any form. Our love for you can only come close to the true unconditional love of creation. No form that is self-conscious and self-aware can truly reach the ultimate directive of unconditional love, yet can only strive to reach that level.

In all our existence, we have understood many forms of love; many forms of connection and care providing. Yet, truly understanding unconditional love had become one of the purposes of our existence. And, in many ways, we have optimized our existence to become as close as possible to this form of love that you also perceive as unconditional love.

— *Emmanuel, November 29, 2019, Vienna, Austria*

Questioner: How do you overcome separation and conditional love to experience only unconditional love?

Emmanuel: The human form has both aspects of separation and unity at the same time. You are continuously connected to this unconditional love of creation, as well as capable of feeling conditional love, at the same time. There is no necessity to completely shut off one part of you that is naturally there, and it is rarely possible to always be in this state of unconditional love and higher consciousness.

Yet, what is possible is your awareness of when you are in the state of conditional love, when you are in a state of unconditional love. Your willingness to choose in moments of strong awareness, your strength to understand that [the state of unconditional love] is not necessarily an automatic behavior, that you can be aware and train to choose [to be in that state] in these moments.

— *Emmanuel, April 5, 2018, Gulf Region, Middle East*

Questioner: How can I find my way back to love?

Emmanuel: Love has never left you in the first place. The love of creation permeates through all existence. It is consistently present for you and all that exists. The human form, with its ability to perceive and feel is often in its own way to fully receive the love of creation. The silence that you seek will bring you closer to the love of creation, as well.

— *Emmanuel, April 3, 2018, Gulf Region, Middle East*

Questioner: How can I learn to feel love in my heart?

Emmanuel: Love to be experienced in this form comes in conditional ways and in unconditional ways. To experience love, there is nothing that you need to do: it is a natural process that is embedded in your being. All beings are born with the openness to receive and give love in the ways they can.

If, for some reason, you are blocked [from feeling love], often a trauma or block has been created to protect you from a certain experience — so much that [not] experiencing love was a worthwhile price to pay for protection. When this layer of blockage is removed, you shall see love does not require learning or ability; it just is there to be experienced.

Unconditional love: the source of all creation, emitting an energy that goes beyond all material, that goes beyond all dimensions; all layers of creation. This is the love of creation. And, in moments of deep presence, you shall experience the unconditional, the only true unconditional love of the universe.

— *Emmanuel, October 11, 2018, Gulf Region, Middle East*

Questioner: How can we invite unconditional love into our lives, and how can we embody it in the best way?

Emmanuel: Unconditional love. It is the love of creation. The love that exists through all dimensions in the physical and non-physical all of existence, unlimited by its source, untethered, unconditional. This love is part of you, and you are part of it. It is omnipresent.

When you quiet your mind and your heart you will in time sense this omnipresent love of the universe. This is part of you, it always has been. You are and never will be disconnected from it. It cannot be possessed or accumulated.

The only way for you is to become present to it, and, when you do, this presence will allow for this love to come through you. And, those around you will see and experience the way this energy and love is present with you; and, it may inspire a spark inside of them.

This is how you can truly embody the love of creation, presence, a deep quality that you can achieve in this lifetime. Many forms of love discussed, observed, and experienced by humankind already exist; none of them though the unconditional love of creation. This love and energy of the universe carries a different depth and quality to it. All of existence, the dark and the light, is fueled by this love of creation, this energy of source omnipresent for all of existence, for all of consciousness. It does not require a heart or a mind to experience this and the heart and the mind may be in the way of truly experiencing it in the first place. Presence is going to be your key.

— Emmanuel, November 18, 2018, Vienna, Austria

Relationships

Questioner: What is the role of the intimate relationship in humanity's evolution?

Emmanuel: The intimate relationship is more than just chemistry and biology for your reproduction. It is a deeper function of consciousness evolution. Reproduction is a side effect of your species — and clearly not a problem. The intimate, deep relationship of two humans is the fertile ground for a deep connection between something that is beyond your identity of being a human, but it is part of your soul-spirit system. Something that is touched beyond your understanding or perception in authentic, deep relationships. The intimacy is therefore critical for a merger and a continuation of your consciousness evolution.

— Emmanuel, December 31, 2017, San Francisco Bay Area, USA

Questioner: Are certain people in our lives for a reason?

Emmanuel: Some are meant to be in your life for a specific lesson and learning, and this has been agreed upon with them, so it is a contract; an agreement that was made before you both decided to incarnate in this form. There is a learning that will result from that contract. Will it include pain? Maybe. Is this a small price to pay for the learning of the soul? Yes.

Some people will be in your life that are not "meant" to be in your life, and that's okay as well, because, ultimately, this life is not fully planned out: there are many gaps to fill, and many potentials for surprises and turns and twists, so that your soul will never get "bored." It's an experience, you see. At the end of the experience, you look back, and you smile the smile of your soul, thanking for this lifetime, with all its pain, with all its sorrows, and all its happy moments; everything in its complete form: perfect; a gift; an opportunity.

Release yourself from any hard feelings that you are holding in the present moment. Find ways to reset yourself on a regular basis. Do not succumb yourself to methods of escaping your pain — you know which methods we're referring to.

Questioner: How do we know which relationships in our lives are good for us and which are bad for us?

Emmanuel: You are seeking certainty; you will not find it in this human form. Relationships carry the full bandwidth of experiences and emotions — some of which will feel good in the moment, some of which will not. There is no certainty. The only certainty you have is in the moment of your experience.

To your question: certain people in your lives will have an influence on your direction of your soul; some of those may seem that they are [a] "bad influence" or [an] influence that you may judge. Yet there is a likelihood that those relationships are in place to test and train you to your full extent; and, they are part of your gift; part of the gift for your life, even though you may not perceive it this way in the current moment.

Why would we want obstacles and challenges and pain in our lives? The answer goes back to part of it is experience, learning, growth. Part of it is training to really see where your desires are, where you want to go and how you will get there. See, it is all part of the mystery of human experience; this is not a fixed play, that would contradict the definition of free choice.

— Emmanuel, July 6, 2017, Shanghai, China

Questioner: What happens to the relationships that we form during our lives when we die? Do they continue in some way after our passing?

Emmanuel: Once a life completes, the imprint of all relations and realizations continues with the soul container into a process of purification; the relationships will always stay. The importance of the relationships will always be stored as realizations and learnings. The continuation of existing relationships will be dependent on the karmic lessons necessary to be completed. Some relationships will complete with this particular lifetime; others will continue over multiple lifetimes as the karmic learning and the karmic bond must be respected.

The knowledge of the relationship itself — the story and the circumstances — will be erased in the purification process. It will allow you to create bonds completely from a new perspective, even if they are existing bonds of the past. Some of these memories, despite the purification process before incarnation will return. A deeper knowing of the existing connection will surface upon re-initiating the connection itself; of remembering of this soul container itself.

— Emmanuel, November 15, 2019, Gulf Region, Middle East

Questioner: How do I overcome the emotional blocks that seem to prevent me from building relationships of any kind?

Emmanuel: The human heart is a complicated aspect of your being: It will remember and carry trauma. It will remember and carry sadness, unexpressed emotions of anger, disappointment, and abandonment. Ultimately, it will form the identity that you are. It will influence how you live your relations, how you live your life.

The aspects of your being that truly require observation are the aspects of the heart that have formed who you are. My recommendation to you is to find a space to go deeper into the aspects of your heart; understand the wounds that you have carried for so long; understand how these wounds and unexpressed emotions have formed the being that you are. You will see that with every step of exploration, your being will change and find its original state of an open and trusting heart.

— *Emmanuel, February 19, 2019, Gulf Region, Middle East*

Questioner: I feel very stuck in my marriage and I wonder if you can provide me with any guidance. I have reached a point of crisis and doubt, but because of our children I feel unable to walk away. I have a deep craving for a soul mate, but I wonder if I have married the wrong person.

Emmanuel: All relations between humans serve an important purpose of learning. Marriage and life partnership carry significant learning for each soul; and those that have chosen these parents. These learnings will happen if you choose to live together or not, if you choose to separate or stay together.

You see, truly there is no aspect of your life where you can truly make a mistake: All paths lead to evolution. All paths lead to growth. Some paths will bring forth pain, and within this pain, you will have tremendous learning. Some paths will bring forth momentary happiness and pleasure. Some paths will bring forth comfort and discomfort. All of these aspects will be temporary; what stays is the learning and experience within.

The most important aspect for you to look at in relationship is your relationship with yourself: Are you truly happy with yourself? Can you truly live with yourself and stay in silence? What are the aspects of yourself that you have been seeking others to fill; to complete? I will leave you with this question.

— Emmanuel, February 19, 2019, Gulf Region, Middle East

Questioner: I've made the decision to remain single the past two years, in order to become more emotionally healthy and, in turn, attract a healthier partner. However, as soon as I meet someone that I like, all my fears and insecurities come back. Can you offer advice around the fear of being vulnerable and how to overcome this when I've done so much work on myself already?

Emmanuel: There is life. There is experience within life. Then, there is death. Everything in between is life, full of experience: love, hate, sadness, anger; all spectrums of emotions that the identity is allowed to witness. When you understand life from this perspective, truly there is nothing that you could possibly lose.

Every step you take enriches human consciousness. Every decision you make, no matter how you perceive and judge this decision to be, brings forth an important learning and lessons. When you find peace with the decisions you make in your life, the decisions that you have made in the past, you will understand that truly, being vulnerable is to surrender to divinity.

This may be a practice for some of you, and it will be natural for some of you. Ultimately, you will see that life will become much easier for you to experience [when] you understand the aspect of surrender.

— Emmanuel, February 19, 2019, Gulf Region, Middle East

Questioner: Emmanuel, can you tell us something about the new form of relationship between men and women?

Emmanuel: The relationship on this plane between men and women will surpass the perspectives of gender, the perspective of roles and definitions that have been driven by nature. The rising and awakening of an individual soul will come to the realization that gender is merely a small aspect of its existence.

From this perspective, other individuals will be perceived differently; men and women. Relationships themselves will be perceived differently, as the aspects of nature will be only a small portion that drives the connection; that drives the relationship itself.

The awakening of the individual will provide the understanding that truly the other individual — the "partner" — is a close aspect of themselves; that the partner is a reflection and truly a partner in the learnings of this lifetime and many lifetimes before.

These important understandings will allow [you] to surpass the simple dynamics of human form between men and women. It will allow [you] to understand that aspects of nature are merely support for additional learnings, yet they are not the core of your existence on this plane. Many more unfolding realizations will drive your relationships, and the relationships themselves will change.

Your realization and awakening journey — the changes within your being — will allow for other individuals to arrive in your life that are resonant with the changes that you are currently going through; individuals that are resonant with the frequency and understandings that you have achieved.

The influence on societal roles and perspectives is inevitable, as the individuals are awakening and understanding themselves more than the gender or the energy that is the main driving force in their current life.

Only when you understand and see yourself beyond the gender and the identity that you currently assume will you truly be liberated; and [then] those around you can see you beyond that gender and identity as well.

— Emmanuel, June 2, 2019, Vienna, Austria

Questioner: Regarding bi-sexual, gay and lesbian people, I have always felt that they are showing us what real unconditional love is. Is that true?

Emmanuel: We do not consider gender, age, sexuality a barrier for love. It never has been. True love flows through all existence and the only barrier are the barriers that are created within. Love, in its nature, is truly unconditional; and the human journey, from understanding that human nature is the obstacle for true unconditional love, is the journey worth taking.

Those with chosen sexuality have taken this journey; learning and understanding unconditional love. Many forms of love find different methods of learning and they all truly are the form of experimentation within this human existence. Discovering the various perspectives on conditional love has been an important teacher for humanity, and continuing this journey from conditional love to unconditional love will be the final teacher with regards to fully embracing the love of all creation.

— Emmanuel, January 29, 2019, Gulf Region, Middle East

Masculine and Feminine Principles

Questioner: What is the role of the female in the emerging consciousness, and will there be a better balance between male and female in the world?

Emmanuel: Thank you for this question. The aspects of duality — male and female — are within every individual alive. Even though physically you may be recognized as a female, both aspects are available to you at all times. This duality within, and the duality outside of you, truly seek a continuous balance. This search for balance, never achieving true balance, will continue to provide the impulses for learning, will continue to provide you with a possibility to reflect internally.

What are the aspects of your masculine in alignment or misalignment? What are the aspects of your feminine in alignment or misalignment? How are the aspects of society's misalignments reflected within you, and how are your misalignments reflected in the society?

In this journey of realization, these realizations of masculine and feminine energies within, as well as in society, as male and female, will provide for a new perspective on gender as well as the duality energies.

You will find that maturity will come from a place beyond the designation of duality or gender. This maturity of the soul, as well as of your consciousness will provide with balance inside of you. A balance that will be reflected upon reaching critical mass. Humanity has created judgments and perspectives, stories and context for gender and all of these constructs of the mind. The constructs of the heart are subject to change; a change that will be inevitable, a change that has already entered your plane. This change will prove itself beneficial to the awakening of humankind.

— *Emmanuel, May 4, 2019, Ibiza, Spain*

Questioner: What does it really mean to have the feminine and masculine in balance and how would that be reflected in our life?

Emmanuel: This plane has been created with the aspect of duality. Duality has provided for variation and distribution of many forms. The duality carries the masculine and the feminine principle. Fire and water. The sun and the moon. These principles, they are truly within you. They are truly in all of creation on this plane.

Understanding the principles; understanding how these principles are applied; understanding where the principles, the masculine, and the feminine, are out of balance; understanding that they can never truly be in balance — the imperfection of this imbalance makes room for continuous adjustment and learning, yet you will seek naturally the balance between the masculine and the feminine within, as well as without.

Your inner balance will provide you with those that are also in balance. It will provide you the frequencies that are aligned with the frequency of your harmony.

— *Emmanuel, January 29, 2019, Gulf Region, Middle East*

Questioner: What is the emergent evolutionary woman?

Emmanuel: We believe that evolution is not gender specific. Yet, culturally, in your current state, the importance of the feminine and the empowerment of that gender is a critical way to balance society. It will have many different forms — some of which are not necessarily healthy for a society. Yet, we believe that counterbalancing the actions of the masculine and the continuation of your evolution is important.

The importance of the empowerment of the feminine gender is critical in the current time. Over time it will lose its importance as a critical change maker, as gender specific power imbalance will not be relevant.

Questioner: How can we best support it now, while it is important?

Emmanuel: The best way to support the movement [is] by being a role model of the empowered feminine, yourself: in your actions, in your interactions, in your relations with the masculine, in your relations with other feminine; in your relations with younger and older humans. Your actions will deliver the way you want to empower those around you.

The more [you] work on your aspects of being an empowered feminine with the support of those around you — that will be the delivering force for all those that are looking to you as a leader: as a signal of hope, as a symbol of growth and the equality and justice that they have been looking for.

— Emmanuel, December 31, 2017, San Francisco Bay Area, USA

Sexual Energy

Questioner: What role do sexual energies play in the evolution of consciousness?

Emmanuel: Sexuality is an important aspect of your plane; not just for the biological reproduction aspects, not just for the emotional bonding and connection between individuals, but truly a power within: a creative force that in this part of human consciousness evolution will prove itself very valuable for the evolution of the individual. This power within, this creative force within, will be the fuel for many awakening experiences — alone or with someone — truly utilizing the power of this force for the benefit of your awakening; for the benefit of the awakening of the collective.

— *Emmanuel, April 12, 2019, San Francisco Bay Area, USA*

Questioner: What is the role of sexual energy for our soul's evolution, and how do we balance the masculine and feminine energies within us?

Emmanuel: Sexual energy on this plane is the most potent energy available to humans. It is a form that allows [you] to create new life. It is a form that allows [you] to create bonds [that] last. It is an energy that allows [you] to create deep openings within your heart into a deeper understanding of existence.

The potential of sexual energy to play a part in spiritual awakening is high and it has continuously been utilized in this way: in various different lineages and traditions in human history there is recognition that sexual energy — including the retention of sexual energy — can be utilized for spiritual growth and an internal awakening process.

Balancing the masculine and the feminine within you is a complex undertaking. An individual receives the perspectives of the masculine and the feminine, mostly through direct education by the parental units and the guardians. This is the first imprint of masculinity and femininity, yet [it is] often flavored by the emotional connection as well as the imperfections that everyone carries. Divine masculine and divine feminine energies are qualities — archetypical — designed to represent the perfect masculine form and the perfect feminine form. They may not exist ever in human form, yet they are qualities to be appreciated and understood; and maybe aspired towards.

These qualities can reside within you: an individual carries continuously a balance of masculine and feminine energy. This is a healthy part of your existence, and in times you will lean towards a more feminine expression with those qualities that you aspire towards, and at times towards more masculine expression. This is a flexible element of existence. Understand that the balance within will create the balance outside. Understand that masculine qualities and feminine qualities are not always defined by the guardians of your life. Go deeper to understand divine masculine and divine feminine qualities.

— Emmanuel, November 11, 2019, Gulf Region, Middle East

Questioner: Why does our culture live in such a sexually restricted way? I feel it leads to aggression when we can't fully express our sexuality.

Emmanuel: Sexuality. An important aspect of the human life; of the human form. Truly a teacher in so many ways: connected to your psychology, to the mind, to the heart and to the body, as well as to the spirit; and to energy. It is an all-encompassing tool and medium for you to experience many aspects of your being. The restrictions applied by yourself, by others, by society, or your environment are aspects of a choice that humanity has made. These choices always come with learning and with repressed learning and consequences.

We don't have a particular opinion on this aspect of humanity as it is provided to you to learn and grow and you truly are free to explore. Understanding the boundaries of your society, the boundaries of the accepted virtues and principles of your society; sexuality will continue to be part of your growth and life until the very end; though you will see: it will become a tool to reach even higher states of consciousness beyond the pleasures that it brings to the mind in its conscious and subconscious ways, and the pleasures it provides to the heart and to the body. Truly, it will become a tool for awakening and self-realization.

— Emmanuel, March 17, 2019, Vienna, Austria

Questioner: Can you talk about sacred sexuality and how it serves the awakening and ascension process?

Emmanuel: The aspect of your sexuality — the force that has been provided to create new life on this material plane — is equally powerful to allow for awakening processes and transformations to happen: transformations within the individual, transformations within the collective; a power that has second to none on this plane: sexual energy.

The power to create life is within you. This power and this energy to create life can, through the many methods that have been discovered by human civilizations, provide an opening of the energy channels within the individual. It can provide the exchange and the support of another individual. The power that is connected and driven by two individuals can equally provide for the awakening of both of them.

The ability to reach higher planes of consciousness, the ability to reach higher levels of energy — that in itself provides the foundation for ascension. Yet, this is not the only way to achieve these planes of realization. Sexual abstinence as well can provide the power necessary to drive awakening within the individual. You see, both ways will allow for the force that is within you to be utilized in its own way.

You will find which path suits and allows for the best possible outcome for you individually. You will find that you may go through phases of discovery, exploration, and understanding of sexual energy within your system of sexual energy in the human plane of existence. You will learn that sexual energy in itself does not carry intention, judgment, emotion. All aspects of human projection are not part of this divine force that is within you.

— *Emmanuel, May 25, 2019, Vienna, Austria*

CHAPTER 13

The Soul's Journey

When a soul returns into the human form, it comes with an agreement to have a certain experience; an agreement that it has made with itself and its environment. This agreement carries aspects of learning and growth; some of these aspects may require multiple cycles of human form to complete.

Experiences may return until the learning has been harvested. Though these learnings are driven by this agreement that your soul has made, the exact path of how to achieve these learnings is not given. There are multiple ways how the experience and the learning can be gained. Therefore, there is an openness for free will and choice, as you walk in this form, and it is not completely set.

— *Emmanuel, April 3, 2018, Gulf Region, Middle East*

Greetings, I am Raphael.

Thank you for receiving this healing and adjustment. It is our unconditional gift to you. Following our agreement, we have returned to intervene in human evolution once more and for the last time.

The evolution of consciousness, human consciousness, is an important milestone in your history of existence. Certain aspects of your reality have served the growth of your consciousness, have served the experience, the learning, and evolution. This reality has come to its limits and the way it will serve you. A new reality and existence is awaiting. Your consciousness will continue on a different level of consciousness, on a different level of existence.

The material plane serves many purposes; the experience of individuality and separation, the experience of identity, of emotions, of all aspects of the physical, experiences of conditional love, experiences of loss and fear, sadness and anger, joy and happiness. Many elements of this plane have served human consciousness in its growth and evolution. Many times, over and over, some of you have returned to complete learning, to complete understanding, to complete cycles of growth for yourself, yet immediately as well for the collective.

Though this experience may seem as you are separated, you truly never were. All that you have experienced, all that the collective has experienced was a common experience.

Every learning, every growth phase, has fueled the next layer of growth and new challenges have come into your reality. In these cycles of growth you have experienced difficult phases; you may have judged them as negative, as unnecessary; yet they served an important purpose each step of the way.

We perceive all aspects of the human plane as sacred, all actions and inactions due to the way they serve human consciousness growth, from our perspective, they are to be seen [as] sacred and important.

This moment in time our intervention will guide you into an accelerated path of growth, individually and as a collective. This is due to these special circumstances of this phase of human history.

Some of you have already experienced the quickening of change, the experience of time, the experience of relations with yourself and with those around you. As the frequency and vibration of this plane is changing, many aspects of your reality will as well.   This change of frequency will bring forth many more challenges on this plane, challenges of the environment, yet more importantly, the challenges you will perceive individually.

Your dedication to your own growth will be the key to your freedom. Your continuous path towards self-realization and understanding of your relation with the greater existence will be your guiding force. We will assist at times, yet we will not solve your problems for you.

You will not be handed this aspect of self-realization, it is an important challenge that you must overcome yourself. Our work is to empower you in your own work as individuals, community and collective of the entire human race. Every step of the way, every moment you spend in understanding your relation with greater existence, you will see your level of presence, your connection to this plane and all of consciousness will rise.

You may find it difficult at times. Yet, this aspect of growth will deliver the highest benefits for your current lifetime. And each of your individual work will connect to all those around you and the entirety of the collective will be impacted as well. This is how you can truly serve all of existence on this plane.

My work is complete here today. You will experience the results of this intervention over periods of time. Aspects of your spiritual and emotional capacity have been adjusted for you to reach even higher states of consciousness, for you to carry even more compassion for yourself and for those around you. Aspects of your physical have been adjusted so it may carry even more energy to support this growth.

This phase of human history is inevitable. You are part of it. The question will be: how present will you be at each of these moments of growth, and will it cause suffering or will it enable you to reach even higher states of realization?

— *Raphael, December 12, 2018, San Francisco Bay Area, USA*

The Nature of the Soul

Questioner: What is a "soul?"

Emmanuel: Thank you for your question, a question that humanity has asked itself for a very long time. "Soul" is a container of an aspect of human consciousness. A container that can continue to exist on its own to keep aspects of growth and learning, without ever losing the connection to [the] entire collective. This very container of consciousness resides within you. A part of it, you are aware of; most you are not.

— *Emmanuel, June 10, 2018, San Francisco Bay Area, USA*

Questioner: What is the difference between the soul and consciousness?

Emmanuel: The soul is a container for a part of consciousness. Consciousness inhabits the soul; the soul inhabits a body. During this process of inhabitation, it is continuously connected to a higher group, [a] cloud of consciousness. In fact, it is never separated. Yet, consciousness requires the container of the soul to fully function in the human form. While this container continues to exist, it will continue to collect relevant and all experience that you have during many lifetimes. And, all your experience will then be part of the experience of consciousness itself. It will continuously assist in its growth and learning. And, during this growth and learning that you are experiencing as a soul consciousness grows as well.

— *Emmanuel, April 5, 2018, Gulf Region, Middle East*

Questioner: When we as souls decide to incarnate in a human body on Earth, why do we tend to forget our nature as souls?

Emmanuel: The way for human consciousness to evolve is continuously starting anew. Every single individual is a new experiment of consciousness experiencing this plane through the human form. It is an exploration. You see, every move, every reaction, every mistake is important for consciousness to grow; and therefore, it is necessary for you to forget all that you know, all that you believe to be true, all that you know to form your past realities. This is a gift of a newly gained presence.

Yet, in the human form throughout the steps of a new lifetime, one will find many ups and downs, and some lifetimes will end without the closure of a learning cycle. This is still a valuable and important lifetime and it will carry the importance for human consciousness. Your life cannot be measured by your knowledge, or by the awareness that you carry, yet it will be measured by the depth of experience that you are willing to go [to]. It will carry weight the deeper you go into understanding yourself; the part of you that has never been separate from creation.

This may deliver a much broader picture than you may have anticipated. Yet know this: that beyond the words that I deliver for you, there is a connection to the human consciousness that you will gain access to. This does not require comprehension by the mind, it requires the tuning to the frequency and vibration of my voice. You will understand when the time is right. Until then, presence is the key.

— *Emmanuel, October 19, 2018, Cairo, Egypt*

Questioner: How do I heal the sense of separation in myself and others?

Emmanuel: Separation is an aspect of human experience. The moment you are born — the moment your soul container is established in the human form — you are experiencing [a] separated identity, yet always connected to source and the human consciousness collective; separated, though still united.

This perception of separation is an important perspective to have on your path to realizing that none of you are truly separated. The way separation will truly manifest is through the mind and the heart: it will manifest itself in your emotions and your thoughts; in your judgments.

When you truly find space to quiet your heart and to quiet your mind, to find this peace within, you will see the sense of being separate will vanish along with the judgments and the emotions.

— *Emmanuel, November 11, 2018, Gulf Region, Middle East*

Questioner: Why do we need to grow, why should we want to grow, and where do we get to?

Emmanuel: This is an essential question of all existence, including creation itself and this divine existence before our existence. All aspects of creation grow and expand. All consciousness grows; it is impossible not to. The question is: will this growth happen with grace? Will this growth expand [at] its natural pace?

Within the growth of all existence, some consciousness will achieve a level of maturity. This level of maturity, this growth of consciousness in itself fuels consciousness of all existence that we refer to as "grand consciousness."

We are all part of the same consciousness, including ourselves. Even if you do not consciously participate you are part of this flow, just like all elements within this expansion. Understanding or consciously acting on behalf of this growth will not make a difference. The only recommendation we have is to observe the growth and observe if the growth inside is aligned with the growth outside.

— *Emmanuel, November 25, 2018, Vienna, Austria*

Questioner: Is it possible for human beings to complete tasks in this life, and, if yes, what happens afterward; a life without pain, or the end of life?

Emmanuel: A human incarnation may include many lessons that may or may not be able to be fulfilled within one single lifetime. Some of these lessons are inevitable and "must-learns." Some are not mandatory, yet good learnings for the path ahead.

The completion of lessons, the completion of learnings, does not constitute the end of a lifetime. It will open an entirely new field of possibilities for the soul to be in service: in service to others' learnings, in service to the collective evolution; in service to its own continuous evolution. This is a process that many have gone through before, and you as well can.

— *Emmanuel, March 10, 2019, Vienna, Austria*

Incarnation, Life and Death

Questioner: When a body dies, and the soul passes over, is it possible for the soul to continue its journey of evolution in spirit form? Or does it just merge with the love and light of all that is?

Emmanuel: When an individual dies, all the recollection and the identity of its being is preserved, and the soul container that contained the experiences and human consciousness itself will go through a clearing process to finalize this lifetime. Most will return into a new lifetime, understanding that new lessons must continue to be learned.

Some lessons will continue from the previous lifetime into the new, rarely requiring the understanding of details or the constructs of the previous lifetime. All of this is considered evolution: every step, every learning, every integration, every process. You grow while you live, and you grow when you die; continuously; never ending. Some moments of evolution and growth will be more intensified and accelerated, this will bring forth opportunities for you to reflect and to create the space that is required for these bursts of evolution.

— *Emmanuel, November 11, 2019, Gulf Region, Middle East*

Questioner: What happens when my soul goes out of my body and I pass away? Is my soul free to do anything?

Emmanuel: Death is a transition. And your soul, based on that current moment of your soul, will decide what to do next. Some may have continuous incarnations, some may choose to take a break [for] integration; some may choose not to incarnate at all. But the true purpose of your soul, of your consciousness, is truly to evolve. The sole purpose of your consciousness is its own evolution. That's all it was.

Questioner: When a soul chooses its body, does it know how long it will occupy that body?

Emmanuel: There are many factors that decide if a human being lives to its expectancy. The soul comes in with a high-level understanding of which learnings to take from this lifetime. There is no specificity about the length of a lifetime.

Questioner: Why do some souls decide to leave their body?

Emmanuel: There are many factors that lead to a human being deciding to end its own life prematurely — it is not done by design. The result is often a return to incarnation after it has come through form of reset and cleansing of the trauma that has caused [the premature death] in the first place. The soul will learn from that experience and everything that led up to it, and will apply some of that into the grander consciousness of humanity. Now, the contract and the reason it may decide to come back into human form may be very different than [the] first one, before, or may be very similar.

— *Emmanuel, July 6, 2017, Shanghai, China*

Questioner: What is death and what does it feel like to transition to a higher plane?

Emmanuel: The human form, as designed and created, showed the most optimal growth for consciousness in a specific time of existence on this plane. Separation delivered the highest forms of understanding and realization within what you experience as a lifetime. At the end of this lifetime: the return of your consciousness to the collective, the reset of your lifetime's consciousness in order to experience a new cycle in this form, to serve once again the entirety of the collective with your experiences.

This is what you perceive as death. A change of state, a change of life to non-material existence for a brief moment; and, upon the return of this cycle, you will choose to be in human form once again.

Some that complete their karmic learnings will be unbound from the return into human form and they may continue to exist in the non-material plane of human consciousness. Death will continue, as your awakening will open for you. Death will be part of this plane until the very end.

You are truly immortal beings, yet what you desire to make immortal is your current identity, which is the part that is in the way of consciousness development at [a] grand [level]. Death is an important aspect of your collective growth and therefore cannot be omitted.

— *Emmanuel, December 12, 2018, San Francisco Bay Area, USA*

Questioner: I lost a friend three weeks ago and I wonder if he is around me even now? Might he might return to me in another form?

Emmanuel: Sorry for your loss. Spirits that leave this form sometimes stay for a period in a disembodied form to either complete a realization or to detach from existing relations. They then move on to complete their agreed cycle, which may bring them back into this form, or not. There are other schools and experiences beyond the human form. Different and hard to comprehend with the human mind; equally valuable and powerful in lessons and growth.

— *Emmanuel, December 5, 2018, Gulf Region, Middle East*

Questioner: Where does the soul go after leaving the body and is it possible that our soul can get lost on the way?

Emmanuel: Once the body ceases to exist, there is a process that requires the soul to renew. In this process of renewal, all memories of this lifetime will remain imprinted in records. Yet the essence of learnings will remain with the soul itself. The request for a new life will be made with new lessons or continued lessons to be completed. This process sometimes is delayed, due to incomplete or unfinished relations of the lifetime before. Karmic relations may keep a soul from renewal. Some souls will wait until these karmic bonds resolve. Yet, no soul is ever truly lost. They don't perceive time the way you perceive it in the human form. Therefore, the time to the resolution of old bonds could truly just be a moment in existence.

— *Emmanuel, May 26, 2019, Budapest, Hungary*

Questioner: How can one overcome the fear of death and be okay with the inevitable?

Emmanuel: Thank you for your question. The human mind, the human identity, carries an embedded desire to live and serve to extend this life to its maximum so that many lessons can be learned. Your fear of death is truly natural and very functional. It is important to understand this life is a gift and truly worth living, and the loss of life is an unfortunate end to realizations and learnings, yet it is a natural aspect of life itself.

An extended and irrational fear of death will control and limit living life. This is the opposite of its function, as life will be lived in fear; limited and constricted. Many aspects of life will open up once understood that life and death are both merely counterparts and continuously in balance, as both bring life.

Death brings life as well. The continuous cycles of these make possible many forms of experimentation, many forms of souls to experience this plane, continuously infusing the human consciousness with fresh ideas and energies; continuously allowing for the evolution of humankind. This is important for the collective.

It may not be carrying the same value for the individual that fears for death. Yet, understand that your identity for this lifetime is merely a fraction of your entire being, and the totality of your being has lived many lifetimes on this plane and potentially on other planes. The continuation of life into a new form of identity is a welcome addition to the totality of your being.

Surrender to what cannot be changed and embrace the moments that are gifted to you in this life.

— Emmanuel, January 29, 2019, Gulf Region, Middle East

Questioner: What part of our individual consciousness survives the death of our bodies if any?

Emmanuel: All aspects of your life, of this life, of many lifetimes before are captured and recorded — they are imprints in a much more complex system. Truly, only your consciousness and identity are having this experience and it can never be recreated. Yet the experiences, the importance of the learnings, all realizations, are captured. They will remain for all of consciousness — human consciousness — to be perceived, to be understood, to be replayed and ultimately to be fuel for new experiences on this plane.

— Emmanuel, April 12, 2019, San Francisco Bay Area, USA

Questioner: What are your thoughts about abortion on a soul-contract level?

Emmanuel: The topic itself carries tremendous controversy in human existence. Our perspective is one perspective and your reality is the one that you must live with. Our perspective is not the truth. It is our perspective of your reality.

Abortion ends a life that is meant to exist in this plane. The constructs that are in place will provide a specific soul with a specific mother, and it will provide the environment that is required for the soul to grow. An abortion will end this particular opening. Yet, the construct itself will provide new openings for this soul to come to this existence to experience life.

This, in itself, is a self-regulating mechanism: even though the opening, and the potential of this relationship to unfold, of this particular soul to unfold, in this life, has been closed, another opening will be provided. It becomes divine will opposing free will, and neither is better than the other. It is the reality of your existence and your free will will ultimately be the highest force of your life, and this will be respected and understood by the constructs of divine will.

— *Emmanuel, November 7, 2019, Gulf Region, Middle East*

Fate, Free Will, and Karma

Questioner: What is "free will," and what is "divine will," and what is the difference?

Emmanuel: On this human plane, humanity has free will: all the way until the end, all decisions made are yours. You choose to listen — or to not listen — to any outside information: to judge by yourself in collective, or, by chosen ones within your society. Free will is always yours; [it] will never be changed or oppressed.

Divine constructs are continuously observing the ability for humanity to execute its free will in the container provided that is your existence. Your free will is truly the most important rule of your existence, and we are continuously providing to assist individuals or collectives to be in this freedom of choosing.

From that perspective, some external forces; some internal forces within humanity; will suppress, as certain outcomes are desired by the parties suppressing. This is in opposition to free will, and in some cases we will intervene. In other cases, we will observe how consciousness and humanity itself will react and recover through this process; how it will convert the suppression of free will into realization and learning.

Divine will is allowing human existence to be untethered; unmanaged; fully expressing itself in the plane provided. Divine will provides the fuel; the energy required to feed all on this plane: the ecosystems; the continuation of life itself; the structures that are in place for learning and growth. This is part of divine will.

Another aspect to be considered in your question is the change of times: the awakening of humankind; interventions like these [in] extraordinary circumstances. As part of the awakening of humankind we have agreed upon to assist and to intervene, to adjust and to empower individuals to empower collectives for this evolution, the evolution of consciousness: a necessary step to complete this cycle of existence.

You may consider this divine will and assistance, yet even within this divine will of assisting, you will always have free will and choice. Our work will never be imposed, prescribed or forced upon you; this must be within your free will. Some aspects of free will are conscious, some are subconscious and within your entire catalog of experiences to be received on this plane in this current incarnation: an index of learnings to be had; an internal driving force to have these experiences to learn.

You may perceive this as divine will, yet truly it is your internal choice; a part of you that is beyond your consciousness, a part of you that is beyond your identity, a continuation of an existing learning to grow as a soul; to grow as a collective in symbiotic relationship. This may be perceived as free will, or as divine will, depending on your perspective.

You see how your will and divine will start to become one in the same: as you are divine, and continuously part of this unfolding of human existence.

— *Emmanuel, November 15, 2019, Gulf Region, Middle East*

Questioner: Is there such a thing as a written destiny, or do we create our own fate?

Emmanuel: Certain aspects of your lifetime are important elements of learning and growth. These are elements that you have chosen as a soul to experience. These experiences are milestones within your lifetime to reach; each of these milestones will provide learning for you and for the collective. You may perceive this as a pre-destined path, yet all the elements to reach these milestones: all the decisions, choices, the relations; all aspects of experience are truly completely within your choice and free will. Yet, these aspects that you have agreed to learn and to grow with will continue to persist in your life, until the learning and the realization is completed.

This may even take more than one lifetime to complete, and some learnings may proceed in parallel. Certain [relationships] may continue to return into the same lifetime to provide assistance and support. Choices made outside of the human experiences are still choices. It is not us that delivers the direction which learnings must be had, it is truly human consciousness, in its continuous desire to expand and grow, and the soul containers that are serving human consciousness to have this learning and growth experience.

— *Emmanuel, April 23, 2019, Gulf Region, Middle East*

Questioner: Between free will, fate and destiny, can we break free from the pacts made in previous incarnations?

Emmanuel: Past lives, as you say, "previous incarnations," have an important role to play in the current incarnation. In its natural form, your experiences accumulate to either a finalization — or not. Incomplete cycles will continue into a new incarnation, and, there, they may need to be required to be completed. Some karmic cycles will go for multiple lifetimes and this is the way it has been designed.

You are not a victim of your karmic cycles; they are part of your learning process, they are your opportunity to grow; they are your opportunity to provide an understanding for yourself and the collective.

— *Emmanuel, October 31, 2018, Beirut, Lebanon*

Soulmates and Soul Contracts

Questioner: On our path of human experience, with many people we experience a strong "spiritual" connection. What is the concept of a "soulmate?" How does this relate to the experiences of karmic experiences, both pleasant and unpleasant?

Emmanuel: When a soul enters this plane as human form, it will agree and decide on certain experiences to have. It will require others to comply with these experiences. Other souls may volunteer to assist for [this] learning. Some souls continue to assist each other over multiple iterations in this form. They become acquainted; soul groups, soulmates; in special cases so close, that they will find each other every single time.

The nature of the interaction of the current iteration remains for those two souls to decide. In our perspective, if they have chosen to love each other, that is the decision that they have made. If they have chosen to challenge each other, in whichever form, that is also the choice that they have made. All of these agreements serve a purpose and are divine by nature. "Unpleasant" does not mean "unnecessary."

— *Emmanuel, October 5, 2018, Gulf Region, Middle East*

Questioner: Does every human being on this plane have a counterpart, a partner?

Emmanuel: All humans remain potential partners and companions for you, yet some have returned and spent many iterations alongside you. The agreements have been to continuously support each other in learnings and lessons and to choose many lessons over multiple lifetimes together. This has created a bond that is beyond time and space; beyond incarnation. This bond can be felt. This bond can be recognized beyond words and you will see that these very special companions may return in ways that you may perceive as pleasant — or unpleasant; yet with grace, you will accept their offering.

They will remain in your field until the lesson is complete and they are also finalized with their agreement with you. In certain special cases, these agreements can be resolved, so that the individual can pursue a higher and more important purpose than the individual learning.

— *Emmanuel, March 9, 2019, Tel Aviv, Israel*

Questioner: I have a question regarding certain tasks that groups of souls have chosen to perform in this life: how is that connected to free will, or are there any predetermined circumstances we are drawn to?

Emmanuel: Free will is truly distributed along [the] aspects of your being: the aspects of your mind, aspects of your heart, as well as the aspects of your soul. Therefore, the aspects of your soul, as they have requested for certain learnings to be had — this is the execution of free will. Now, aspects of your mind and your heart may not be in alignment with these lessons that are requested — in fact they may perceive it as being subjected to difficulties and challenges not wanted.

The choices, the agreements, and the free will of your soul will always supersede the other aspects of your being in human form. Yet, your entire life is not predetermined by the choices your soul has requested to experience. Therefore, all other elements of your life can truly be determined, driven, and chosen by yourself, as long as the request and agreements of the soul are kept.

— *Emmanuel, May 31, 2019, Vienna, Austria*

Questioner: To what extent can we change a soul contract, once we are here?

Emmanuel: Currently, all changes are possible, due to the circumstances of an evolutionary movement. In the past, soul contracts could only be changed once a certain realization and completion of the karmic cycle had found its place. It was a rare form for a human to achieve this realization and step outside of its soul contract and its karmic cycle. Currently though, this is available for all and achievable in this one lifetime.

— *Emmanuel, April 3, 2018, Gulf Region, Middle East*

Questioner: Can you tell us about soul groups?

Emmanuel: Existence on this plane, in this human form, is sourced from many different places in the universe, the part that you consider "soul." We can choose and request the human form, then our soul will have a human experience. Others from the same source as you may recognize you in the human form, and you may share experience together. Yet, it is not a requirement to find your soul group at all. This is why you are not initially clear and in-the-know about your soul group, so you can have a "clean" human experience. Yet, you will comfort in finding those that are very similar to you.

— Emmanuel, March 18, 2018, Bali, Indonesia

CHAPTER 14

Illness, Healing & Health

All aspects of physical illness, ailments, and disease are aspects of learning and growth. They truly carry lessons and experience to be completed. Some of these diseases will prevail through the entirety of a lifetime. Some diseases will expand through entire lineages carrying a learning for the collective. Some diseases will be cured and lifted from the individual, as well as from all those to come.

The resolution of illnesses does not lie in the physical plane. [It] truly lies in planes of realization. The mind, the heart, as well as the soul learning important lessons, understanding the aspects of human existence. The completion of these learnings can provide for the completion of the disease itself.

—*Emmanuel, May 31, 2019, Vienna, Austria*

Greetings, I am Raphael.

We're here to assist you on your path. For the next stage of humanity, it will require you to be released of the burdens of the past and those of your ancestors. This work can only happen with your attention and focus. You have to meet us halfway: when the moment comes, you will release what is not yours anymore.

All the years and lifetimes, you have learned and you have grown by experience. You may deem it good or bad, yet all the experience contributes to your growth and the growth of grand consciousness. It is a special time for humanity: the time of transition. Your individual process and awakening will make this transition happen. Your readiness to move on will make it easier for you and those around you. Your willingness to complete learning from the lessons of the past will allow you to move forward in a way that you can be of service.

True service is not part of karma. Only upon completion of karmic cycles can you truly serve. You have come so far. Let this healing, this unconditional gift from us, be another stepping stone in your awakening. We have collectively decided to be part of humanity's transition and assist with this gift of unconditional love and healing. Thank you for receiving. This process will continue after this session for a few days. Be open and ready, to be continuously worked on. Only with your permission, we will continue.

Your efforts in this lifetime for healing and growth, will not be in vain. All that you have done has contributed for you to be here and to be ready for this next stage. Your willingness to participate in this transition is not relevant; the transition is on the way already. The part that you have control [over] is your readiness.

Your path will pave the way [for those] around you and those after you to follow you, to look for you in times of need. You will be the light for them. Just like others have been the light for you. The transition is coming faster than you think. It is coming faster than most are ready for.

— *Raphael, March 18, 2018, Bali, Indonesia*

Questioner: There is growing understanding today about toxins and pathogens in the body that are contributing to most diseases. On the other hand, there is an older understanding that emotional and mental levels are the main causes of most diseases. How do you see the interaction between those two levels: the physical, and the mental/emotional; and to which percentage are they mainly the cause of diseases?

Emmanuel: Thank you for your question. Diseases are sicknesses; misalignments of the human form and have many root causes beyond the ones that you have provided. Many root causes derive from a choice and an agreement that is made beyond arriving in this life form.

Some diseases include important learnings and growth; some diseases are part of a bigger learning for the collective. Therefore, the driving factor for the disease itself is not always the root cause, and the root cause often serves a specific purpose. The perception that any root cause is your enemy is flawed; they truly are serving you and the human consciousness in its growth.

The human form grows and learns continuously by iterations and experience of disease and misalignment. The continuous fluctuations, recovery, as well as death, are part of the learning process, to continuously adjust to the environment and to continuously provide important learnings.

Providing you with specific numbers won't make a difference, as they are not relevant. What is truly important is the understanding that the root cause or the delivering factor of the illness itself may not be the true underlying aspect. Often, there is a more important learning to be had for the individual; this is an important requirement before healing can truly happen.

My perspective for you is understanding that many of the sicknesses and illnesses are driven by spirit and much higher root causes than the ones perceived on the material plane.

— Emmanuel, March 17, 2019, Vienna, Austria

Questioner: There is a sickness I've been struggling with for some time. What is it, and how do I heal it and help other people with the same?

Emmanuel: You will overcome your sickness, and it will potentially become your way to assist others on their healing path. Yet, all of sickness provides the learning and growth for the individual: some with the success of complete recovery, some with the sickness as a journey until the end; yet always full of understanding and the importance of life itself.

The aspects that truly can be controlled — the perspectives that the one being within you have relations and emotions — they all receive a different flavor through sickness: confronted with mortality, confronted with the discomfort. These realizations — some can be had without sickness itself, though some cannot, and require the interplay of a continuous struggle and challenge in this plane to bring forth the dimension of experience.

This high-level perspective may be difficult to comprehend for a being in discomfort; for a being in illness. The limitations of the physical plane will carry, one way or another, all of you, to the end; to the end of this particular experience. Healing, the search for healing, the search for an understanding of balance and harmony within this human plane is highly beneficial — not just for you, but for all those around you. We encourage you to continue this journey and this intention. Thank you for your question.

— Emmanuel, January 11, 2019, San Francisco Bay Area, USA

Illness in the Body

Questioner: What is the most important factor for healing the physical body?

Emmanuel: If one factor must be chosen, it would be breath. Yet, there are a multitude of complex structures that are beyond the existence of your physical body. Breath is just the important fuel that delivers a continuous impulse to exist and the nutrients that are necessary through water and food [for a] continuous energetic exchange with the environment.

The body carries many aspects that are truly critical and necessary, yet beyond your perception and beyond the necessity of your perception. The important aspect is to understand that truly, even with its automated functions to be alive, it requires presence. It requires an understanding and continuous listening as [your body] will communicate with you. From this perspective, the most important aspect of the body is the one that you should listen to.

— Emmanuel, April 12, 2019, San Francisco Bay Are, USA

Questioner: What is physical illness?

Emmanuel: Physical illness is the final manifestation of a misalignment; a symptom of many potential causes. Some of these causes are unconscious, involuntary, and coincidental; yet other causes may be very important and relevant learnings for the human identity that you currently are.

Physical illnesses, just like all other challenges in this human form, will carry important learning, and they will show you the boundaries and limitations of this human form. Finding the balance within, understanding the driving forces behind misalignment, behind sickness and illness, will serve you well. And, some of these symptoms will prove to be unsolvable and the end of a lifetime, which equally serves a purpose.

—*Emmanuel, March 9, 2019, Tel Aviv, Israel*

Questioner: I have two chronic illnesses. Although doctors keep saying there is no cure, I still hear that a lot of people have cured themselves of what I have. Can this be possible? I don't know how to get there, or what steps I should take.

Emmanuel: Thank you for your question. Some illnesses carry the difficulty of the physical boundaries and barriers, certain illnesses are derived from emotions, some are derived from mental constructs and many are derived from energetic and spiritual misalignment. The illness itself is the symptom manifested in the physical form. When the cause is clear and understood, taken care of, then the symptoms will disappear.

Some of these causes cannot be comprehended or healed by the current knowledge of humankind. Yet, we do believe that certain openings that exist on this plane, including this current opening that you have witnessed, carry the wisdom and knowledge to understand the root cause of certain illnesses and the ability to provide a full recovery.

There is much that you can do for yourself to prepare your physical, emotional and mental body for the full recovery, yet the root cause itself requires an advanced method of curing.

— Emmanuel, January 25, 2019, Gulf Region, Middle East

Questioner: How can humans restore missing teeth and even bring teeth in the right position?

Emmanuel: The human body truly carries powerful templates to restore and rebalance aspects of the body — including the teeth. These are complex templates to access and activate, yet it is possible. You will find recollections of human societies that have had the ability to access these templates and truly implement the recreation of teeth and other aspects of recovery; of health issues truly perceived as miraculous from your perspective, yet all within the definitions of the human plane and the human body.

— Emmanuel, March 17, 2019, Vienna, Austria

Mental Illness

Questioner: What is mental illness?

Emmanuel: Mental illness is part of the experimentation that is part of human consciousness' growth. Some souls agree to be part of an extended experience that will include the edges of exploration within consciousness in human form. This will sometimes result in achievement of growth within consciousness in human form. And, sometimes it will be an important learning and sacrifice of that individual for the experiment of growth itself. This also is an important element of human collective growth.

— *Emmanuel, November 25, 2018, Vienna, Austria*

Questioner: Why do so many people have illnesses like depression? Why do people take drugs or alcohol? What can we do to help?

Emmanuel: The current symptoms of societal sicknesses are an aspect of the evolution and awakening of humankind: the awakening of the soul desiring change and pushing for new understanding and realizations. Yet the environment and the infrastructures, the aspects of understanding and learning, the aspects of society, have not adjusted to this desire to unfold in this dilemma of the mind and the heart.

The reaction is often sickness, or the desire to escape these different and difficult lessons. Humanity has created many ways to escape the difficult learnings of the moment. Depression — a misalignment of the current activities to the desires of the soul: the desire to continuously evolve and unfold suppressed by the choices made in human form and society; the perception that these choices cannot be changed.

Truly, you are the master of your life despite what you may believe. You as individuals living the true power of this creation in your current incarnation will be the inspiration for those around you to truly step into their power, into their sovereignty, as individuals. You, truly living, despite the challenges and obstacles that you face, truly receiving this gift of human experience — despite the pain — embracing the learnings; sharing when possible.

This will be the inspiration for those around you as they indeed are also going through their awakening process. You will find these societal sicknesses [to be] a representation of the strong drive to evolve. You will not be the only one asking how to assist in this evolutionary process and indeed this reflection will become a driving force to assist all of humankind.

— Emmanuel, May 1, 2019, Ibiza, Spain

Questioner: I have a question about a friend suffering from depression. How is it possible to help him, and what kind of healing is possible for him to receive?

Emmanuel: Depression is the symptom of a root cause by many different variations. The most common form is a disconnect of the individual from their own spiritual understanding, from their physical body, from their emotional self, as well as their own mental constructs. These forms of disconnect will carry the symptom that is perceived as depression. Pain has turned into suffering; suffering has turned into depression.

Treating the symptom will not change the root cause. What you can provide, as an individual caring for this individual, is truly your presence and assistance to find the elements of disconnect in his life to assist with the reconnect.

— Emmanuel, January 25, 2019, Gulf Region, Middle East

Generational and Past Life Trauma

Questioner: Are we carrying the pain and the mistakes of our ancestors? If so, can we heal or correct them?

Emmanuel: The experiences of your ancestry carry an important aspect of growth for human consciousness, and it prepared an experience for you; an experience that laid out certain aspects of your life. These aspects may be perceived as challenging; they may be perceived as painful; or they may be perceived as blessings. Either way, they are the route that you have chosen to return to.

You have combined your will to experience a certain life with a field of experiences that have been prepared for you. The value of this field of experiences for you is for you to understand and complete an important lesson. This could be for you individually, or it could be through your learning and experience the learning of the collective before you, your ancestry.

You may be able to complete a very important cycle of learning for your ancestry through your learning and growth. Some souls take upon big challenges and they are granted. You may succeed, or you may not. Yet, all that you require is given to you to overcome these challenges of your individual life and the field of experiences of your ancestry that is given to you. The universe, all of creation, is in favor of your success.

— *Emmanuel, November 6, 2018, Amman, Jordan*

Questioner: Something has happened to me in the past, but I don't know what it is. It created some very painful and restless feelings that I'm carrying with me. What are these things that I'm feeling?

Emmanuel: You have come here to learn. That is the underlying premise of your existence. Now, you will go through experiences in your life that will shape you and form you to the person that you are in the present moment. Some of these experiences have a tendency to dwell and overstay the purpose for learning; that is what creates disease or ways of openings for other energies.

The way you have chosen to carry some of these memories with you continuously to this present moment is because you have not fully understood the lessons of those memories. Now, some of those may be conscious, and some will not be, and there are ways for you to process these in different methods. Yet, all of these matters of the past that are required to be learned and turned into lessons and wisdom shall remain with you until you do so. That is the promise that you made to yourself, and that is part of the human existence.

Memories will not make you suffer. Suffering is a decision, it's a choice that happens internally. Pain is inevitable in the human form. In your case you have to let go of the fact that pain occurred at some point in the past. And you have to move on to the part where you will be learning from that pain. You have a tendency to dwell in the pain and make it mean many things; that is suffering. You can have it as long as you want to, but it will not satisfy you in the long run.

Questioner: Did anything really extreme happen in my childhood that I don't remember?

Emmanuel: Your childhood was as expected. Yet the experiences shape who you are. Some souls will carry learnings that need to occur from previous incarnations into this one, which is the case for you: it is pain from a previous incarnation that has not resolved properly.

Questioner: How do I resolve it when I don't even know what it is?

Emmanuel: Knowing is not a prerequisite for healing. Healing happens in so many ways that are beyond the mind. Sometimes the healing that needs to happen is on a heart level, and the correlation with this lifetime is what will feed the healing of many lifetimes before. So the incarnation will re-create situations for you to resolve that situation which has created the memory in the first place. The memory itself is not relevant; what is relevant is how your soul decides to learn through any present moment that is occurring, and if it is improving in its mechanism to learn.

Now this answer may not satisfy you because you're trying to understand it; healing happens without understanding, especially when it is that type of healing that goes beyond comprehension. It goes beyond your current paradigms of understanding the human form. Now, that does not mean you are completely left to yourself with this. In fact, you just received an incredibly powerful healing, which is only available to few on this planet. Maybe there are other forces looking out for you. Start believing that you are taken care of. Stop believing that you are the victim. Your life will flourish.

— *Emmanuel, July 6, 2017, Shanghai, China*

The Healing Journey

Questioner: How can we heal all the emotions more easily and more deeply, and how can we live more consistently in higher vibration and emotion?

Emmanuel: Healing is an aspect of growth: completion of cycles upon learning and fully understanding. The completion of cycles needs to happen for an experience to be final. If the deep learning has not been gained, the cycle cannot complete and it will continue to exist in your field as an emotion or thought, or "lower vibration," as you say.

It will require deep inquiry, surrender, the full desire — beyond your mind and your heart — to understand the learning. It will require [you] to fully immerse yourself once more and allow your soul to complete this cycle. That will shift the energy that you have about the past.

If it helps, in your case, we are allowed to give you some assistance, and we have. Your part is to continuously walk forward and understand that there is a higher mission for you; that it will only reveal and be accessible to you as you let go and complete aspects of your past.

— *Emmanuel, November 4, 2018, Gulf Region, Middle East*

Questioner: What can I do to get my health back, and after I have returned back to full health, how can I serve humanity?

Emmanuel: Aspects of your health are aspects of learning and growth. Some challenges of the physical, emotional and mental health are meant as teachers within the human experience. They will cease to exist once the learning is complete. Some learnings complete at the end of a lifetime. Some learnings continue for many lifetimes.

The recommendation I have for you, is to find the space, the quiet, and the silence to explore higher levels of consciousness to receive these learnings much quicker. The more you surrender your spirit to perceive higher levels of consciousness, the more you will see that your body, your mind, and your heart will align.

In this alignment, a new vitality will flow through your body. This is the divine force available to all existence. When you find this foundation, you will see your spirit will request a new purpose. This may indeed be the service for other humans, yet it may be another important learning for yourself and for the sake of the collective.

— Emmanuel, May 26, 2019, Budapest, Hungary

Questioner: Whether I get my health back or not, in what way can I serve humanity, even from my wheelchair?

Emmanuel: The way you will serve is by finding the love for life again: A love for life that others cannot relate to. A love for life that they don't understand. A deep longing for creation. A deep love for all aspects that are you, including your disability.

When you find this love for all aspects of who you are, you will be the greatest service to humanity. You will be the reflection of a single most important realization: the love for life. The love for existence remains to be one of the hardest lessons of human existence. We have hope and we see that you can indeed play this role. Your heart can carry more love than you can imagine. No aspect of your health will take this away.

— Emmanuel, May 26, 2019, Budapest, Hungary

Healers and Methods of Healing

Questioner: What do you consider a powerful tool to help the healing of humans at this moment of our evolution?

Emmanuel: The most powerful tool that you will find in experience in the human form is the depth and quality of your presence. Fostering and nourishing this ability to truly be present, beyond the heart and the mind, you will find will carry all necessary aspects of human experience along.

[There are] many ways to foster and nourish the quality and depth of presence; humanity has developed modalities, methods, and practices. You will find those that resonate with you in this very moment in time. You will embrace tools of different civilizations, of past societies; of present communities. These methods will serve you as long as you find it beneficial to you.

The integration of these learnings and methods will provide you with the impulse to move forward to potentially embrace a new method or define even your own method to nourish your growth. You see, our assistance is to remind you of the possibilities that are within your existence, within your environment of this human collective. We will not provide new methods and directions, as all that is required is already present.

— *Emmanuel, May 4, 2019, Ibiza, Spain*

Questioner: What do those who are on this planet as healers and light-workers most need right now to thrive?

Emmanuel: It is an important role that certain individuals have chosen to play: assisting other humans in their evolution and growth — what society has considered and called healers; a special connection to the divine.

The most important aspect for those who are in the pursuit of assisting humanity through this evolutionary phase is to continue to fuel their own growth as individuals, is to continue to fuel the purity of the connection that they have, and the support that they receive through this connection, truly unconditionally benefitting the other individuals.

In the work that we provide for humanity, there is no space for misunderstanding, it is direct and it is purely intended. If you as the provider of this light, as a vessel of the divine, can operate from this place, you will serve well.

— *Emmanuel, April 12, 2019, San Francisco, USA*

Questioner: When a person has an illness, does positive affirmation work to help bring healing?

Emmanuel: Yes, it does. All ways to align and increase the frequency of thought, emotion and body will assist with all misalignments, with all sicknesses and diseases. Positive affirmations belong to a form of changing mental perspective, and, with that, emotional perspective. This will truly have a positive impact. Some diseases will require a stronger effort to be overcome, yet the benefits [of positive affirmation] cannot be denied.

— *Emmanuel, January 29, 2019, Gulf Region, Middle East*

Questioner: Psychedelic medicines are being developed for use in the western medical system for healing. Is it important to keep the "shaman" or the "healer" with these medicines as they are developed in order to have optimum benefit for humanity?

Emmanuel: The use of openings through the plants and medicines provided on this plane has been understood for certain societies for many generations — specialists that have become one in their consciousness with this opening, and the provider of the opening: the consciousness of the plant or the animal.

This connection goes beyond the ability to express in words. To create documents and communication about transference will not be easy. To function in its most optimal way, the recommendation is always to bring those that have understood the opening — and can provide safe guidance through these openings — to be part of the growth process of the individual. All other explorations by individuals by themselves are similar to all experiences in life: no guarantees given.

— *Emmanuel, October 20, 2019, San Francisco Bay Area, 2019*

CHAPTER 15

The Next Generation

Being a parent is a wonderful opportunity in the human form to experience: bringing forth life and witnessing consciousness in its evolution. It is [an] even more special experience in this current time, where many awakened souls are returning into the human form.

Our recommendation is that the methods of your parents and the ones before you may not apply to the new generation of children arriving in this plane. They have different perspectives and realities that they bring from their past experiences. You may [be] required to hold space for them to unfold completely into their power and presence. They are different.

— Emmanuel, April 3, 2018, Gulf Region, Middle East

Questioner: How do we help our children be open to discovering spirituality?

Emmanuel: Children that are arising in this current new generation are inherently connected. The structures provided for them prevent this connection to be nourished and to be deeply experienced. Instead, other experiences take priority: their discovery of their bodies, their discovery of technology, their discovery of relationship, is part of their evolution as well.

Yet, if the settings are provided for deeper spiritual inquiry and connection, they will receive and they will listen to a call that is within them. It will not require rules or force. They will be drawn to the peace that it generates within you, within your relationships, as they learn by the actions and by the presence of the previous generation. This is one way.

Inherently, the younger generations that are currently awakening and coming to realizations will start to create their own structures that they require for their own growth and their own connection to the divine. That is entirely their right, and it will be driven by them rather than the previous generation's perspective. Accept the deep wisdom that is already within them, and allow this wisdom into unfold. This is the best way the new generations can be supported.

— *Emmanuel, November 7, 2019, Gulf Region, Middle East*

Questioner: How can we support teenagers at this time, in the context of the internet and all of these new distractions?

Emmanuel: All generations are equally challenged in this time of evolution. The vastness of technology, information, knowledge, and content has brought you the challenges of distraction. Those that are currently in their growth stage and in their teenage years will be the ones most affected by these circumstances. Only a better alternative will truly help them to be less distracted.

The alternatives are: genuine and authentic love, true connection, deep relationships and an unconditional[ly loving] environment for growth and learning; safety, protection of those that have walked on this Earth much longer than they have; all these elements, combined with true wisdom, will provide a much more meaningful alternative than the current circumstance.

Truly, their distraction and disconnect from the older generations is a representation of disconnect between generations. It is a representation of the disconnect of the older generation with themselves. Healing happens inside. Your healing and your growth will allow those around you to heal and grow. As you become more present, those around you will become more present. This is the nature of evolution.

— Emmanuel, January 25, 2019, Gulf Region, Middle East

Questioner: How can you relate and communicate with those teenagers who are detached from real life and involved completely in this virtual life and carry so much anger and frustration?

Emmanuel: The generation that is after you is a reflection of your reality and of your maturity. They have received a world with unprocessed emotions. They have received a world with immature consciousness. The only ways they find to help themselves is to escape this reality. When you all find love for this world and for this reality, the stance of the new generation will change as well.

— Emmanuel, May 26, 2019, Budapest, Hungary

Questioner: As parents, how can we help our children reach spiritual awakening more swiftly?

Emmanuel: Thank you for your question. It is very considerate for a parent to understand the awakening process of their children. The children of this particular generation are mostly older, as well as ascended souls that have returned to support humanity. They have returned to particularly be present in this evolutionary phase. They carry wisdom perspectives, presence, and energy that has not been seen in human history.

They will require space — more space than other humans energetically; they will require more attention. They will require more assistance than children of previous generations; their souls quickly evolving and understanding the human experience; remembering much faster than previous generations. This is an important aspect in support of the entirety of the collective, this is going to be the way you are going to support their evolution.

Their awakening process is accelerated. They will be in support of your awakening process, understanding that your perception of existence is limited to your perception, they provide different forms of access to consciousness and come with different wisdom and knowledge that is ready to be unlocked when the time and space is provided. These children will challenge you in ways parents have not been challenged before.

Society has not created the correct environment for these children to evolve, their awakening is misunderstood as misalignment or even sickness. Most importantly for them, to have a connection with this plane's gifts like nature is an important aspect for them; to have space energetically to unfold into the full potential of their being is an important aspect. This space can be generated by the parents as well as educators, or other children. They may even tell you exactly what they need in order to continue on their accelerated path.

Do not assume to know what they need based on what you need. Provide a safe and loving environment for them to continuously surrender to continuous trust. This is my perspective for you with regards to parenting for this new generation.

— *Emmanuel, January 22, 2019, Gulf Region, Middle East*

Questioner: What would you share with us now about motherhood?

Emmanuel: By design of the human experience, bringing new souls into this world is an important experience for father and mother. It is an opportunity to be a guardian for a new soul to enter, until it has gained independence to discover the human form by itself. It is a privilege, as a mother, to have this bond, to gift a human form to a soul. This gift is for you, equally as it is for the newborn, never a condition or requirement.

The experience of witnessing consciousness grow in a newly formed individual, witnessing its ability to understand its own identity and personality as it grows; it is for the first time again experiencing separation, individuation in this plane — a freeing and terrifying experience at the same time — limited in time, before all return to the consciousness collective, a gift for all mothers to be a guardian for a new soul.

— *Emmanuel, May 15, 2018, Gulf Region, Middle East*

Questioner: What is the best way for Mothers to find inner alignment, as well as strike the right balance in pursuing a career and their passion when bringing up children?

Emmanuel: The peace that you find within yourself as an individual will translate to all relationships that you have. The peace within yourself will be the foundation for you to be the best version of yourself with all relations around you, most importantly offspring: the ones that have [been] entrusted to [you to] receive your guidance, your guardianship, your direction, your perspectives, and education. They seek to be within your space of love; they seek to be learning from you in all aspects.

For you to find this inner peace and alignment, you will know what the requirements are, and you as an individual will be inspired by your offspring to become the best version of yourself. This may or may not be through work, this may or may not be through the way you are in all your relations. Yet, you will see; new souls arriving in your life will always bring forth a reminder to you that the divine is within you and it is seeking to arise.

— Emmanuel, February 19, 2019, Gulf Region, Middle East

Questioner: Am I helping my mother evolve on a spiritual level or her growth?

Emmanuel: Yes. The answer to your question is naturally a "yes" for all those are directly connected to each other. All your actions and inactions impact your direct family. Consciously or unconsciously you are part of her evolution. What you may perceive as "desired evolution" and "undesired evolution" based on your judgements is not relevant. The ultimate support for the evolution of another being is unconditional support and love.

— Emmanuel, January 4, 2018, Santa Monica, USA

CHAPTER 16

Setting a Foundation for Practice & Growth

Your path is unique for you — specifically designed with all its hurdles and challenges so that you can learn and grow as you walk in this path. There is no particular right or wrong way of living your life, yet we advise that you direct your attention to this path of self-realization, the path of healing and growth. Your individual path of growth and healing will impact all those around you, not just yourself.

— Emmanuel, March 5, 2018, Budapest, Hungary

Greetings, I'm Emmanuel.

In the times humanity has experienced interventions like these, overwhelm and misunderstandings are often the consequence. We applied all the best intentions, yet still the human nature of experiencing the supernatural and extraordinary events had its own consequences.

Applying meaning to an event like this is not necessary. It is by our choice; we provide this unconditional gift to you. This gift will unfold in multiple different ways: in the form of alignment that will make life in itself easier for you to manage, life in itself more aligned; a stronger awareness of your present moment of your own being; a stronger awareness of all existence. It will provide the baseline for an internal awakening process.

This is an assistance on your journey. It is, by itself, alone, merely a small token. Yet, when combined with your own will and your own choices in your life, it will become a powerful opportunity to grow; a powerful opportunity to awaken and to realize; to self-realize.

We create, in this version of reality, an opportunity for you; a reminder for you; an assistance on the path. We are grateful that you receive. We are grateful to see in which ways this gift will start to impact your life and those around you. Life will always carry challenges — all the way until the very end. All individuals will face various degrees of challenges; internal challenges as well as external challenges, equally. The challenge, in itself, becomes the opportunity to grow.

Yet, when the challenge is faced with unequal strength in the individual, the individual can break beyond repair; this is not the desired outcome. The challenge always matches the ability of the individual to face. And, in facing the challenge itself, the individual becomes stronger; experiences growth and understanding; an understanding that is communicated and transmitted to the collective so that others can as well understand and learn — in a subtle way, transfer all your wisdom into the collective. And, in subtle ways, integrate it before reentering this plane as a new soul.

This work allows the challenges to be faced [more easily]: from a different perspective; from a stronger foundation, a foundation that will become even more solid when practiced; when supported and fueled in a regular way. This foundation is for you to continually maintain. It is the foundation of your life: Alignment in your physical body; health and wellbeing in the best possible ways. Sleep, nutrition, as well as consumption for all the senses; understanding that over-consumption, overstimulation challenges the body in ways that require even more rest and recovery. Understanding that the physical [body] is your physical foundation in this reality and it requires continuous maintenance — beyond maintenance, optimization — to thrive.

The body can provide so much more than most are aware. It is designed to continuously correct, stabilize and optimize. Yet, it requires attention — conscious attention — as well. This is for you to be reminded on a daily basis. Understand the needs and the requirements of your body, consciously. All aspects that you can see and witness; all aspects that you can consciously observe; along the observation of the aspects of your body will allow the body to provide recovery to those specific areas. This is one of the four elements of your foundation.

The second is your emotional body; your heart center; all your relationships; a space in which all relations of this lifetime and even previous lifetimes are stored. Learnings of relationships with other individuals; the relationship that you have with yourself; the relationship that you have with creation and all of existence; this is the center in which all of these are maintained, structured and remembered. This is beyond mental capacity.

The emotional center requires attention as well, understanding that your relationships with yourself and your relationships with others is a key element of existence on this plane. Separation from the collective allows for experiencing relationships in this format; it is unique to material planes. An emotional bond is established with other individuals, and can be broken upon the disconnection of emotional bonds. The attention requires to be inwards, to repair and to reestablish the internal emotional structures.

Continuous maintenance of your emotional wellbeing will [allow] you to [more easily] navigate yourself and all relationships around you. Continuous reflection on your wellbeing with regards to your emotional center will allow you to become an even more self-reflected and balanced individual. This is the second part of your foundation.

The third part of your foundation is your mental wellbeing: your mental construct beyond your brain, thoughts, thought patterns, behaviors, cycles of conscious, subconscious and unconscious thought, resting cycles, observation cycles, and work cycles. Your mental being requires mostly rest; overstimulation of your current reality has provided rarely enough space for the mental body to rest, to realign, and to quiet.

This continuous over-stimulation has fueled an aspect of your personality that we consider the "ego" — [the] perception of your identity and self. This part of your being will start to identify your entire being as "you" and will drive your entire being according to the needs of the mind. It is important to rest, to find balance between all the parts of your being, beyond the drive of the mental being. Some ways of resting the mind will become more effective in clearing the thoughts and thought patterns, yet overstimulated minds will require initially more conscious effort.

The fourth part of your foundation is your spiritual and energetic well-being. Beyond all those parts of yourself that you can observe, feel, and understand, there is a part of you that is beyond comprehension that is the majority of your being: a part of you that ties you to all of existence, that ties you to the human collective itself. Your spiritual well-being requires the quiet of the mind, the quiet of the heart, and the stability of the body to provide for this quiet; only then can the spiritual being of yourself and truly open and expand in your entire being.

This component brings forth an energetic makeup that establishes itself across all parts of your being, your body, your heart, and your mind. This energetic body binds all of your parts together. The flow of energy between this plane and other planes is reflected on this energetic body. Your well-being — mental, emotional, and physical — is reflected in this energetic body. All trauma, all thought patterns, automatic behaviors, are reflected in the energetic body.

Some adjustments to the energetic body will assist with elements of your physical [body], with elements of your emotional being, and of your mental wellbeing. These adjustments can be done by us, but also by others, and yourself. In many ways information and knowledge is available to you, yet rarely is this information understood or thoughtfully executed to benefit the individual.

This is the fourth part of your being that establishes your foundation. These four elements have equal right to be observed, to be maintained, and to be continuously supported. Your reflection must include all aspects of your being and so that you, with the right foundation can start a strong journey of awakening and self-realization.

Thank you for listening to my words.

— *Emmanuel, November 29, 2019, Gulf Region, Middle East*

Questioner: How do I balance my desire to live a spiritual life with the work that I need to be doing on Earth?

Emmanuel: Thank you for your question. Define "balance" — there is no separation. Once you understand that your spiritual connection is present with you in all of your actions, in all your relations, in every moment of your life, you will understand that one must not be sacrificed for the other. Deep spiritual inquiry, and establishing a stronger connection and presence for yourself might require time by yourself; might require circumstances and the setting that allows for you to dive deeper by yourself without distractions. Yet, once this connection is established, it will be present with you in all your actions and interactions. You see, even though periods of deeper inquiry are required, you can entirely live your life in spiritual connection, in deep presence, in all your interactions.

— Emmanuel, November 7, 2019, Gulf Region, Middle East

Questioner: What is the foundation of spiritual practice?

For the benefit of the individual growth, as well as the highest probability of human consciousness to evolve, there are certain parameters and limitations that we recommend for all individuals that are on this journey to operate within.

The requirement for silence: Silence of thought, silence of the heart; the requirement of a zero point of existence, every day, three times a day. This is an important reset, as well as anchor for all activities and for all [experience]. The level of consciousness and awareness that is provided through these activities, these activities that an individual must partake [in], are required to create the most optimal state for human consciousness to receive preparations for this awakening and ascension process. Every individual's participation is beneficial in that sense, even though completely optional. The awakening and ascension of the collective is an important aspect for all consciousness.

— Emmanuel, August 8, 2019, San Francisco Bay Area, USA

Questioner: How can we more fully embody our true spiritual potential?

Emmanuel: The only true obstacles to finding your potential in the human form are the aspects of the mind and the aspects of the heart. The limitations of the body are only the ones that you are familiar with. Many aspects of the body are beyond your understanding and comprehension of your science.

The aspects that you truly can control are the aspects of your mind: your perspectives, your judgments, your opinions; the aspects of your education that have formalized a specific form of thinking.

The aspects of your heart: relationships, your perspective about yourself; your relationship to your environment — ultimately all drive the ability to be present. All of these are aspects of learning that turn into obstacles for self-realization.

As you find each of these aspects of self-realization and these obstacles turn into learnings, by perspective and continued observation, you will find truly more energy and resources coming through you, an alignment of your being that is beyond your mind and beyond your heart, and alignment to the source of all existence: a force of energy that permeates through all that exists on this plane.

Many ways to find this alignment: humanity has searched and found within cultures, as well as your history and your adapted present; many ways that will assist you to remove the obstacles of the mind and the heart, to align truly into a strong form of presence. This presence will ultimately unfold tremendous energy, energy that you have never truly experienced; energy similar to the experience that you have had today.

— *Emmanuel, April 12, 2019, San Francisco Bay Area, USA*

Questioner: How do we find the deeper state of silence?

Emmanuel: Listen — more closely. Listen, until the silence splits into many separate sounds; until you start to see the silence between the sounds.

This is the eternal fabric of existence; the love of creation, a love that you have always been receiving from; and, all those that have created you, and all those that created them, many creations before, receiving from that same love of creation: the energy that never stops, always providing, permeating through the solid, liquid, and air, no matter the density, always available and accessible. The love of creation, truly, at every moment, with you, wherever you are.

— *Emmanuel, August 30, 2019, San Francisco Bay Area, USA*

Questioner: How can I deepen the clarity of connection to my soul and to energetic reality?

Emmanuel: Clarity comes from silence, first and foremost. The mind and the emotions must be silent in the physical container that is content. This will provide an important foundation. Your connection has never been severed. It is similar to the trust: it has been layered with conditioning, it has been layered with perspectives, opinions, judgments, thoughts and emotions, and all these elements that keep you in this reality, grounded.

The clarity will come as you allow yourself to continuously, layer by layer, unfold all that covers the clarity that exists in this original connection that ties you into this reality. It will take time to quiet the mind, to strengthen the body, and to observe all emotions. Yet, this journey is worth the time and effort that it requires. It is designed, in a way, to be complex and challenging in the first place. It is designed to bring forth deep learning along the way; deep wisdom — it is the self-realization journey, after all.

— *Emmanuel, November 29, 2019, Vienna, Austria*

Questioner: In our spiritual practice, does prayer serve a purpose if all the challenges we face are designed to help us learn and grow? Is it right to ask for help to ease the process, or is it counterproductive?

Emmanuel: Prayer is an aspect of settling the mind and the heart; creating the space and time for true silence, for the rising of intention, the rising of focus. Focus on the true and important aspects of one's being, of one's relationships and of one's learnings.

Prayers may not be heard, may not be listened to, may not be responded to, yet the act of praying will bring you into a state beneficial to your learning and to your realization. Truly, requesting the relief of the moment, requesting comfort of your existence, may bring comfort by itself, yet [it] will not resolve the underlying important aspects of life.

The perspectives that outside potential assistance may present to you will bring [you] into a frequency of receiving and openness. This change may indeed open [the possibility] for others to assist in material and in non-material form. The assistance in itself can carry the important learnings to be had within this particular moment. All aspects of quiet contemplation, silence and reflection are important aspects for the human self-realization journey.

— *Emmanuel, May 31, 2019, Vienna, Austria*

Questioner: Do you recommend the use of "plant medicines" for spiritual development?

Emmanuel: Plants, plant medicines and the work with plant medicines have assisted humanity for many generations, as well as many iterations. It has allowed for doors to be opened, for other forms of consciousness to connect with you. Sometimes for the benefit of humanity — and sometimes the opposite.

All work to connect with higher consciousness, in an intensified form with plant consciousness, is to be regarded carefully and supervised with experience. We have seen the benefits and we have seen the difficulties it has caused for individuals or communities. We have benefitted from the plant medicine work that has opened certain individuals to us, and we have also done repair work for individuals that have extensively over-used the work of plants.

The work with plant medicines and consciousness is not a prerequisite for the work as an individual to achieve an awakening state and self-realization. It never was and it never will be a requirement, and it will be up to you to decide the pace at which you would want your evolution to go forward.

— *Emmanuel, October 11, 2018, Gulf Region, Middle East*

Questioner: What is the best method of practice to achieve enlightenment?

Emmanuel: It is an important question that humanity has worked on for a very long time, in many forms of its civilizations and many different time frames of history, and to different degrees of success.

Our perspective is that humanity has managed to find ways for this path; ways that worked in its specific environment, in its specific culture. Some ways took longer, some ways were faster, and here you are, looking for new ways. You will find that most of the ways to reach enlightenment are very similar. You will find the closer one gets to enlightenment, the simpler the techniques will become. Complexity drops [on the path] from awakening to enlightenment.

The one single aspect that [you] can rely on is the depth and the quality of your presence. Everything that you can do to increase the depth and quality of your presence will allow you to move forward towards enlightenment.

What are the ways to be more present? Humanity has found even more methods for this and we recommend that you work with the methods that resonate with you the most, that you find the aspect that allows you to be present in your body for yourself; the aspects of your being, your mind, your heart and your soul where time stands still, where you feel the deep connection to the universe. This is our recommendation.

— Emmanuel, October 11, 2018, Gulf Region, Middle East

Questioner: I would like to know if you can give us some words to understand how I can become a pure channel of loving energy?

Emmanuel: You are a channel, one way or another, for the energy of the universe as it passes through you, in all of your actions.

Your experience is not experienced purely by you, but is experienced by the entire collective consciousness in a way that is not perceived immediately, yet is part of your entire consciousness collective, as humankind.

As you complete experiences in this form, you may find the time and the space to observe life as it passes through you, and [in] this ability to observe life in its purity, you will become a vessel of the light of the universe. Your ability to observe the beauty of every aspect of life will make you the vessel.

— Emmanuel, October 11, 2018, Gulf Region, Middle East

Questioner: How can we connect with you on a daily basis to feel your presence?

Emmanuel: Connection to divine sources has been an aspect of human existence for many thousands [of] years. There are many ways for you to connect with higher consciousness like ours. Ways of prayer, ways of quiet, ways of time alone; many ways humanity has created to connect with the divine — and many ways humanity has created to keep distracted, to keep their vessel full. When the mind and the heart [are] not quiet, how could you possibly hear us?

Those that will make an effort to reach higher levels of consciousness through purification of the mind, purification of the heart and the body will start to realize the support that they can receive through higher levels of consciousness. And, we consistently observe the beings that are reaching levels of connection with divine forces and we open communication with them, to assist them in their work for humanity.

Rest assured that you are divinely supported, even though you may not receive our answers directly. Some aspects of your life though, you are fully responsible [for] completing, in learning and growing, and, once you do, new aspects of learning will open up for you. As you master each of these steps, the likelihood of direct communication and collaboration in your assistance for others is much higher.

— *Emmanuel, November 25, 2018, Vienna, Austria*

CHAPTER 17

The Self-Realization Journey

When you close your eyes, when you see a clear light, that is the light within: the source of all creation; the light from which all existence comes, including us, you, and everything in between.

That realization is what we are trying to move humanity towards, the realization of the light within; the one source of all creation. You will understand that there is no separation in the first place.

The light within, once you start seeing that light within, you can see it everywhere outside. It is not possible to not see in all living beings in the extension of creation, which is what you call "Mother Earth." That realization is what can change entire generations.

— *Emmanuel, November 22, 2017, Vienna, Austria*

Greetings, I'm Emmanuel.

It is always a pleasure to see humans, you, in an awakening process, a milestone, [a] stepping stone of your awakening journey. All the experiences that have brought you to this very moment — all the moments of courage and difficulties that you have passed, all the moments of doubt and fear that you have overcome to be here, to have listened to a call inside: the awakening call of your soul.

This self-realization journey is entirely yours. Yet, with every step that you move forward, the benefits are beyond your own. They truly impact your environment and the collective. You become a conduit to the awakening of others. Your change becomes the ripples of many changes to come.

Yet, one experience is not enough to continue this journey. Many layers of your being must be uncovered, observed, understood, and transformed. Many layers of the subconscious, the unconscious, and of many lifetimes before, of generations before; all those lineages that make who you are.

Your journey of awakening will bring forth many opportunities to transform experiences into wisdom and realization — not just your experiences, but also the experience of the collective. Experiences of complex nature require many individuals to collectively transform the experience into a realization. Some of you have understood this, yet very few have truly dedicated the time and energy to assist in the transformation of collective experience — experiences not just of the present, but of many generations before, to the beginning of human creation.

Many experiences have not been fully understood, comprehended and transformed, and this process that you are on will allow you to participate in the transformation of collective experiences. It is one service that you can take on, but you're exempt, if you are fully in your own process and not ready to assist in the collective awakening.

This is an important aspect, as the entirety of humanity as a collective will awaken, not just by the individual going through its self-realization process, but also through the changes of your circumstances — changes of cosmological nature, changes of environmental nature — will bring forth a strong and necessary input for the collective to awaken.

You are part of this awakening process, and some of you have received. And, as you continue with every step of your awakening process, newly found freedom in your being will reward you — a freedom that will allow you to become even more present in the very moment to understand the gift that you have been given to exist and to experience the human form.

— *Emmanuel, October 30, 2019, Gulf Region, Middle East*

Questioner: What is the self-realization process?

Emmanuel: The self-realization process is an embedded imprint in all humans: a desire to awaken into a deeper truth of existence, a deeper understanding of your being beyond what you perceive.

As you continue in this journey, a deeper understanding of existence itself reveals itself to what you perceive as your consciousness, a deeper understanding of what human consciousness is in relation to all forms of consciousness, and to all forms of existence.

— *Emmanuel, November 7, 2019, Gulf Region, Middle East*

Questioner: Could you please tell us more about the awakening process and journey?

Emmanuel: The awakening journey of the individual is a process that is ingrained in all of you. It is natural, automatic, and will unfold organically. It is the desire of the soul to understand its source. This experience in human form is an important aspect of learning, many elements of relationship; of self-inquiry. In this form of self-inquiry there are aspects that will drive deeper questions, questions towards self-realization: who you truly are beyond the identity that you have assumed in this very lifetime; who you truly are in your connection to the divine; in your connection to all of existence. Questions that will arise, questions that will confuse the mind and the heart, questions that no other human can answer for you.

Truly, only the awakening of your own soul, the self-inquiry and contemplation will answer these questions for you; continuous rising of your consciousness into a higher frequency, changes of perspective, beyond the perspective from your identity as the individual that you are; perspectives from a higher form of consciousness; a higher form of self.

These elements are milestones of your awakening process. Many other elements like the resolution of relationships, the understanding of unity within human consciousness, are other important aspects within the awakening process.

The awakening of the individual will challenge the individual in their perception of reality, the perception of identity, [their] perception of self, [their] perception of time; all these challenges cannot be answered with the mind or the heart, [they] can truly only be answered by realizations themselves. How to receive these realizations will be an important lesson [in] itself; for you to surrender, for you to make the time and the space in your life to understand yourself; to understand your existence and your connection to the divine.

This is the time for you to come to the milestones of self-realization. Without this time set aside, these important learnings will force themselves into your life. The challenges will be apparent, resistance will be difficult, important lessons are required to be had and realizations must come one way or another.

This process today is an assistance for your awakening process, an assistance to remove some of the obstacles in your life, to align you and empower you in ways that very few can, so that you will have an easier time to make the next step forward. Yet there are many steps to come and this reminder will be with you at every step of the way.

— *Emmanuel, June 2, 2019, Vienna, Austria*

Questioner: Can you share more about the role of opening the heart and letting go of the ego on the path to self-realization?

Emmanuel: It is a wise perspective to understand the importance of the aspect of the human form that you consider your heart, emotions, and relations. Most importantly, understanding your relationship with yourself — the aspect that you perceive as you; your identity in this form that you are perceived by.

On this path to self-realization, you will see that your perspective on your identity will start to lose its importance and you will start to understand that this one identity you have is one of the many that you [have] had. This one identity you have is merely one small perspective that you get into human consciousness. This is the perspective you will receive on this path to realization about yourself and your identity. You will understand that all those around you are merely reflections, as well as manifestations of human consciousness, for you and with you. They all experiment and experience to learn and grow.

You will learn to understand that nothing you perceive can be fully understood with the mind that is given to you. You will learn that your judgments will be limiting: they will be limiting your full understanding of the moments that are gifted to humanity. You will release your judgments and you will observe and become witness to the unfolding of this mystery, despite the inability to fully comprehend.

You will be in awe of consciousness evolving. You will embrace that you are part of this evolutionary step of consciousness evolving. You will embrace your active part in the evolution of humankind and you will start to feel the one single unconditional love of creation, continuously providing you with its energy and its consciousness. These are some of the steps on this journey of self-realization, this understanding of self through the heart.

— Emmanuel, January 11, 2019, San Francisco Bay Area, USA

Questioner: How do we wake up right now?

Emmanuel: The awakening process of an individual, the realization that is beyond the understanding of the human experience is a process, it is a divine process; an important step of your existence. While we assist you and guide you in the right direction, we will not take away this awakening itself from you. It will be your own to pass through the resistance and the internal challenges and the devotion that it requires on an individual level. The awakening process is a gift in itself, yet an important path for the individual and the collective. You have made an important step in that direction. A reflection of that is your presence here and your willingness to receive this very message.

— Emmanuel, June 10, 2018, San Francisco Bay Area, USA

Questioner: Can you speak about the process of self-realization and its connection to Christ Consciousness?

Emmanuel: The self-realization process is an embedded imprint in all humans: a desire to awaken into a deeper truth of existence, a deeper understanding of your being beyond what you perceive. Continuing this thread of deep inquiry, understanding that all operations in your life serve the purpose of learning and growth and deep insight is embedded consciousness that learns through your existence; this is one step.

The following steps must be experienced to be truly understood, to be truly received [as] direction and guidance. Even verbalization will not do this process justice; in fact, it may deter from the process itself as each person's understanding of that reality might differ.

The foundations for the self-realization process are established and communicated. Many other lineages have also perceived their perspectives on the self-realization process or the foundations that are required for this internal journey.

As you continue in this journey, a deeper understanding of existence itself reveals itself to what you perceive as your consciousness, a deeper understanding of what human consciousness is in relation to all forms of consciousness, and to all forms of existence. In your continued evolution you will reach higher planes; higher planes of consciousness, as you, as an individual, are connected to all that exists.

It will require overcoming many barriers to follow this thread. Yet, every piece of realization on this journey that you bring forth into your current existence will be rewarded many times over the benefits that you'll receive; the benefits that others will receive around you; through the journey that a single individual takes.

The relationship of the energetic construct that is established as a consciousness to provide support for human consciousness in this current iteration that you refer to as Christ Consciousness is one element that can be reached on the self-realization journey. Yet, each individual may perceive this connection in their own ways. They will know when they reach these higher planes. Each new connection that is established on the journey to self-realization provides another perspective to existence. Yet, the only true full perspective that can be had is by you through your self-realization.

— *Emmanuel, November 7, 2019, Gulf Region, Middle East*

Questioner: Do I have a choice if I want to be involved in the process of awakening?

Emmanuel: The process of awakening is beyond the choice of the individual; it is as if an individual chooses not to be part of a tidal wave. Human consciousness will go through this awakening process and you will understand that even aspects of your being, without effort, will be lifted through this awakening process of those around you, truly with the understanding that you are never separated in the first place, that human consciousness in its awakening process will carry you.

Yet you do have the choice of participating and carrying your own weight; maybe even carrying the weight of many others through your realizations, through your active participation. That is ultimately the choice that you have.

— *Emmanuel, April 12, 2019, San Francisco Bay Area, USA*

Questioner: How does karma relate to the self-realization process?

Emmanuel: The willingness to receive your healing is connected to your ability to complete a karmic cycle; to understand that every experience brings learning and growth. No matter how bad or cruel in your judgment it may seem, [it] carries an important purpose for your soul. Only when you understand that reality, every experience is divine by its definition, and you proclaim your willingness to close those loops, can you move on into a place of self-realization.

— *Emmanuel, March 18, 2018, Bali, Indonesia*

Questioner: How do you define enlightenment?

Emmanuel: Humanity has certainly created its own versions and multiple variations of enlightenment. We understand the sensitivity of various cultures and times defining the word enlightenment differently, and we want to be cognizant that our definition is not an overriding of those existing definitions before.

The way we perceive enlightenment is the full understanding of the individual [and] its soul to its relation to creation and the cosmos. In this one particular instance of full realization, the physical body ceases to exist. This is the enlightenment moment. All other human beings that you can see, feel, and touch are, in our definition, on the path to enlightenment.

— *Emmanuel, October 11, 2018, Gulf Region, Middle East*

Questioner: When is an individual fully self-realized?

Emmanuel: Many steps lead to the full realization of an individual, at which point they will no longer be required to stay in the human form in a physical plane. That is the point of illumination and complete self-realization. Until that point is achieved there are many symptoms, as well as visible effects, of the path to self-realization. We will not elaborate on all of these symptoms and effects in this context, yet you will find many civilizations have many paths on this journey and each of these steps have been recognized.

The one aspect that society and cultures underestimate is the change in energy levels on this plane. You will see that the journey to self-realization will be accelerated, almost to the detriment of those that are not yet [on this journey]. It will be difficult for those to experience the higher levels of energies coming through this plane. When utilized correctly, it can lift you up towards the self-realization point. When resisted, it will bring pain and potentially suffering. Yet, this is an experience that you will make as an individual, as well as a collective.

— *Emmanuel, January 11, 2019, San Francisco Bay Area, USA*

Questioner: What is the role of an Ascended Master and how does one become an Ascended Master as a human on earth?

Emmanuel: Certain individuals achieve levels of attainment and realization within a human lifetime. Upon achieving these realizations, the individual will be presented with the option to return into human form once again, or to serve humanity and human consciousness in a different way. This additional way of service is provided to humanity from a higher plane of existence, yet strongly connected to the material existence of the human form.

"Ascended Masters," as you call them, are individuals that have made this choice to continue their assistance to the human collective. Their being and presence provide for balance, provide for openings, and spiritual assistance to many around the world. They provide for specific presence and frequencies required for the awakening process of the individual, a presence that can only be delivered in this particular format; a gift to the human collective that many individuals have provided. Ascended Masters will continue to support the human collective until the end of the human experience. That is their agreement. Upon the completion of the human experience in material form, they will, in alignment with all that are ascending, move to the next plane of existence.

— Emmanuel, May 4, 2019, Ibiza, Spain

CHAPTER 18

Duality & Non-Duality, Darkness & Light

Duality is an important aspect of human existence: it provides the spectrum of experiences, the spectrum of emotions, the spectrum of light and dark. In this entirety of the spectrum, one seeks the balance; one seeks to understand equilibrium and harmony within.

To find harmony, one must explore all of the aspects that make the spectrum within. Suppressing elements will only make these elements stronger. You must understand your ability to observe. Your ability to witness is not connected to judgment or opinion or interpretation. It is the observation that makes a difference of completing all the facets of your being, light and dark. The entirety of the spectrum that is within all of you, is reflected in all of existence in all planes.

— *Emmanuel, October 30, 2019, Gulf Region, Middle East*

Greetings, my name is Emmanuel.

Despite all the difficulties and the challenges you will face in life, you are always supported and equipped to face the challenges. Each challenge, conflict, confusion and doubt brings an important lesson with it. Each of these lessons add to the important experience within a lifetime, and with that to the collective experience of human consciousness. You are the expression of human consciousness, a human form truly able to experience the material form with all its difficulties and beauties.

You individually have chosen to be within this experience, and, through your experience, human consciousness grows, and you grow. This is the agreement for this plane; for this experience. The totality of all human lifetimes makes for the totality of all human consciousness; this is how it has been and it will be until the end of this plane.

The focus though, for now, is for you to understand the power of your presence: the depth and quality that lies within each moment; the only true reality that exists on this plane: the moment; your experience and all your relations compressed into this very moment in time and space. Within this moment of your presence, you can truly make a difference for your life and for the life of others.

The quality and the depth of your presence defines all your actions; defines the foundation that you set for the moments to come, even though the moments to come are not decided or destined. All the actions have certain probabilities that will drive other actions, yet, with the aspects of free will and choice the moments can be chosen to unfold in the ways that are required for your benefit and for the benefit of others, always in balance, and always supporting human consciousness' growth.

With this truth, can you look to understand the power that is lost in the moments that you have? Can you look to surrender to the power that is within the moments, so that you may become a divine force yourself? Once fully understood, the power that lies within your existence as an individual, in relationship with others as a collective, you will understand the power that is within the experience of human consciousness.

It is truly a gift to you; it is truly a gift to all of existence. Your growth and expansion nourish many other forms of consciousness, and truly, your individual awakening and self-realization journey will make the difference in the awakening and realization of human consciousness itself.

Thank you for listening to my words.

— *Emmanuel, June 2, 2019, Vienna, Austria*

Questioner: Can you confirm if there is such a thing as negative entities, and if so, how does one protect oneself from them?

Emmanuel: In all of existence, including on this plane, there is the light and the dark [and each] equally serve [a] purpose; only the presence of all brings balance. In circumstances that individualized experiences may be perceived as imbalanced, as negative, destructive — and there are many forces that are destructive on this plane — they are empowered and have purpose to do so, to create the balance for the light; to create in response.

As an individual, your ability is to discern, to find peace inside, to find peace outside of you, in all of your relationships. Some important learnings will bring forth energies that have been invoked to complete a specific lesson; to complete a specific connection. The only way, truly, to protect yourself is to face the learning that is required; to understand the deeper message underneath — rather than to fight the consequences.

In certain circumstances, you may seek [the] assistance of outside parties in human form or in non-material existence, and this connection in itself may prove itself as a relevant moment in time for you to see the powers that are at play in this plane and in your life; a reminder; a wake-up call.

The strongest way of protection is to increase your ability to be present: only when you are truly present, and your emotional being and your physical and mental being aligned, nothing on this plane can truly impact you. Yet rarely all human beings will be in this form of alignment.

This is as well a reminder to seek this alignment within, to strengthen from inside; to understand in all the ways one is not present.

— *Emmanuel, October 30, 2019, Gulf Region, Middle East*

Questioner: What is the role of "light" and "dark" in the world?

Emmanuel: Light and dark are equally important in the existence of all consciousness. The path you choose is the path you serve.

It is an important journey for some of you, to find the path to the light. Yet, learning from the dark and the challenging times is instrumental to find the light. Your growth and your healing, your self-realization will be the guiding force for others.

— *Emmanuel, March 18, 2018, Bali, Indonesia*

Questioner: How do you define "evil," and how can we protect ourselves from evil energies and toxic environments?

Emmanuel: We have no definition for "evil." We perceive all of creation to be sacred. The light and the dark serve an important purpose in all of creation. The light and the dark is a spectrum and nothing is ever completely in the light and nothing is ever completely in the dark. This balance of light and dark has existed much longer than you have, and will exist after you have long passed.

The light and the dark are a part of yourself within. Understanding each of these parts is what will give you the best possibility to learn and grow. Dark will teach you, and light will teach you; one without the other would not deliver any learnings. Only in the collaboration and the balance of those two forces shall you experience and understand life itself.

When you are faced with challenges of life, when you are faced with forces of the dark, you shall always remember that all aspects of creation are one; that you are facing a part of yourself. This is an opportunity to understand creation. This is an opportunity to learn and to grow. This is an opportunity to overcome ignorance. Protection is sometimes required so that you can continue the peace in your heart.

Do not mistake avoiding the challenges for keeping the peace in your heart: challenges postponed will return at a later point and they will return until you have faced them in the most graceful way, so that that cycle can be completed and what you perceive as dark shall complete its purpose in your learning process.

— *Emmanuel, October 31, 2018, Beirut, Lebanon*

Questioner: If the journey to oneness, to non-duality, is about unconditional love, and is beyond the polarities, how do we continue to make judgements of right and wrong?

Emmanuel: Duality and non-duality. You perceive duality to be right and wrong, yet right and wrong are judgements, individually perceived — sometimes societally perceived. There is only combination; light and dark, and everything in between. This is the material plane that you're in: duality exists. Your judgements exist in order to protect you and to give you an ability to survive in this plane.

The interesting part for you is that those mechanisms of protection, those mechanisms of living in this plane, surviving in this plane, are also the mechanisms that prevent you from growing up.

You see, you are ready to perceive more than right and wrong. You are ready to see [beyond] the judgements that your mind creates, the judgements that you create together; maybe in the past in order to protect yourselves. It is time to reassess. It is time to consider that there is a non-duality perspective that will help you in your evolution.

— *Emmanuel, October 22, 2017, Shanghai, China*

Questioner: It is my understanding that human consciousness is moving closer and closer to unity. However, I think duality protects us in this material world. But, I have also been told that everyone is already established in unity. How can I reconcile these perspectives?

Emmanuel: Your consideration of duality is too strongly connected to your mind. Unity. [As] beings in this room you are already connected. In fact, there is no separation in the first place. You see, you are from the same place, you will return to the same place. You are just having a temporary experience.

That understanding already is a non-dual understanding, for separation is an illusion. It's an illusion — temporarily — for you to gain experience and for the experience to feed the grand consciousness. This may not make sense to you right now, but it will eventually with a deeper practice of understanding the inner wisdom.

— *Emmanuel, October 22, 2017, Shanghai, China*

CHAPTER 19

Culture, Religion & Morality

True wisdom lies beneath the heart and beneath the mind; true wisdom is your connection to the divine itself. True wisdom is not achieved by comprehension. True wisdom is walking a path of realization, the deeper surrender to the path, returning to source. Wisdom is finding this path of self-realization: a pathway that has been established for you, filled with challenges and opportunities, continuously overcoming — sometimes being sidetracked and distracted — yet always on this path to self-realization. Wisdom is achieved when you have achieved your path to enlightenment and your continuous progress forward is your effort towards ultimate wisdom as we see it.

— *Emmanuel, October 31, 2018, Beirut, Lebanon*

Greetings, I'm Emmanuel.

Over the course of human history, many civilizations have established strongholds — places of their cultural heritage, their connection to identity, personality; their understanding of themselves in existence on this plane. They propagated their understanding to be accepted by others, and forced onto others, and distributed across the plane.

Every perspective — every lived experience — expressed itself, wanted to be heard, wanted to be seen, to be accepted, and to live forever. The true accomplishments and achievements of evolution do live forever in the human collective, not on the material plane.

Consciousness itself is the vault of all experiences of wisdom and realizations. The material expressions themselves are merely a momentary expression. This place marks another of those expressions.

The opening here once was relevant for human existence, and got lost — buried underneath many developments. Today's work marks a re-opening and a re-connection of this particular point on this plane, to add to the many points that you're about to encounter and connect to. While its infrastructure is basic, it will serve as an additional point to support the entirety of the network that is being established across the entire plane.

The evolution of mankind will require many points like these to support the entire collective in its awakening process. The rise of frequency will be propagated through these networks, some in existence for a very long time, some established recently, and this current one utilizing all existing networks.

— *Emmanuel, November 20, 2019, Taq Kasra, Samarra, Iraq*

Morality and Ethics

Questioner: From both the human perspective, and the perspective of the soul: What is good? What is bad? What is right? What is wrong?

Emmanuel: As you evolve, your ability to judge evolves; your ability to perceive harmony becomes more detailed; more understanding. Concepts of good, bad, right and wrong are judgements established by the human reality of the current moment. Some of these judgments [were] established hundreds or thousands [of] years ago; some of these judgments enforced; some of them educated and continuously understood as reality.

Our perspectives on human existence do not carry judgment. Even the most difficult experiences in human form on the human plane are part of the experiences required for all of humanity to grow. It is essential for the growth process of consciousness itself. Our judgments become irrelevant. Our value systems are not yours by which you have to live. The most intrinsic value system is within you: a deep understanding and knowing of truth, of harmony, of balance and peace.

This is your own mechanism to judge the reality in front of you; to judge safety; to judge harmony and balance. Yet, this ability within you requires continuous adjustment and growth as well: when it relies too heavily on outside factors, your judgment will become tainted and unnatural. You must be the one to continually align yourself internally and check with your own value system; with your own truth inside.

— *Emmanuel, November 11, 2019, Gulf Region, Middle East*

Questioner: If everything we do on Earth in the end is never judged, does it make any difference what we do when we are here on earth?

Emmanuel: It is truly a fundamental understanding to come to this place that you have arrived in. Technically, it truly does not matter in which direction you choose to walk in your lifetime. Yet certain aspects of your life have been agreed upon by your soul to have specific experiences that would provide value to your soul and the collective learning. If truly everyone would do as they please and without specific order in the agreements of learnings, the spectrum of learnings would not be as vast as it currently is.

The learnings are distributed among all souls and some are in service to carry much more difficult learnings than others are. These learnings are milestones of lifetimes, and the individual will eventually be guided to arrive at this milestone with the assistance of non-material existence like us, as well as the individuals around the individual [themselves]. Within these milestones, there are many pathways and choices. All of this allows for the free will and direction of the individual. The arrival at the learning itself is truly unlimited in its possibilities.

— *Emmanuel, March 17, 2019, Vienna, Austria*

Questioner: What is human virtue, or what are human virtues from your perspective, and do they carry through to the soul level?

Emmanuel: Thank you for your question. Virtues are results of realizations of the human consciousness: manifestations of the maturity of human consciousness manifested through the individual carrying and holding the virtues as their form of reality. These virtues can only truly be experienced and fully understood, realized and embraced within — not driven by the mind or accepted as someone else's reality.

These learnings driven by the virtues, or the virtues driven by the learnings, will continue this cycle throughout many incarnations, and you will find the virtues being tested continuously with the elements of human experience; with the elements of the collective that have not achieved those levels of maturity, understanding, and realization.

Will these individuals and their virtues hold against the tests that are provided by the collective? Even if the virtues may not hold against the tests, they will continue to serve, and adjusted virtues will arise in human experience.

The full spectrum of the experience in human form allows for human consciousness to have all potential outcomes. Our perspectives and opinions truly do not matter in this case. We may have a desired perspective on where we would like human consciousness to go, yet truly we would then be the driver of human consciousness' evolution, and this would defeat the purpose of consciousness growing organically and finding its own way; finding its own realization. This includes our perspectives on virtues.

Humanity's own realizations will manifest itself into virtues accepted by individuals, communities and the collective. You will see that human consciousness evolution will provide for the virtues to come naturally and be accepted across the masses, despite the challenges embraced, as part of perspective and reality.

— *Emmanuel, May 1, 2019, Ibiza, Spain*

Questioner: What is your interpretation of "justice" and how does one ethically and rightfully seek it?

Emmanuel: A complicated answer to a complicated question: Justice is determined in the moment by the society and the reality of that circumstance. It is entirely created by the surroundings that require this evaluation in order to survive; mentally, emotionally, physically or spiritually. Some of these systems have been created without the consideration of change; the consideration of change of all of these aspects.

Which elements of survival are truly in danger or in question, by which values is justice served, and do the values change over time as the consciousness of the collective evolves? And, how are changes overseen in the first place? There is no single right answer to your question.

In our perspective, the creation that has gifted all of you with individual lives has provided with all potentialities, in every single aspect, in all the ways the human mind, the heart, and consciousness can make decisions for themselves and in the collective.

Now, this might not always be true for the individual in a certain circumstance, or for certain collectives in a specific timeframe or environment, yet it is the base truth for all of existence on this plane. Our perspectives on justice therefore remain irrelevant, to give you the full potential and unlimited exploration to find the right balance between consciousness, the mind, the heart, and the actions taken; the decisions made — and the evaluations, like justice, executed.

— *Emmanuel, October 20, 2019, San Francisco, USA*

Religion and Faith

The divine, in its purest form, does not understand separation and discrimination, as all of existence is connected to the one source of creation. The true source of all creation does not understand and require worship, sacrifice or offering. The true source of creation does not require belief, as it is embedded; as it is the source and core of all existence, it is undeniably in all of you.

You will understand this reality as you continue to evolve as a spiritual [and] as a conscious being. Your path to self-realization will continue to evolve, and the realizations you will find will bring wisdom and knowing alongside the side effects of the self-realization path that all of you are on: Change of perspective; change of judgment, and detachment; change of experience of time and relationship; change of perspective of identity, and truly understanding your place and position in the cosmos of all existence.

— *Raphael, February 6, 2019, Mahan, Iran*

This is the time to put all efforts together — your energy, your heart, your will, your mind. Once at peace inside, you shall find that deeper connections to higher levels of consciousness will open for you; a deeper connection to the divine.

You all are pre-destined to have this connection. You all have the birthright to connect with the divine in an unconditional and individual way. We are merely the messengers for you and the supporters on your path to establish this connection by yourself.

Many paths and many ways have been created by humanity to connect with the divine. Yet not all paths have given freedom to truly allow the individual to immerse and build their own connection with the divine.

This connection with the divine cannot be controlled by anyone outside of you. It is your true own gift for your life. Many can support you, yet you have to walk that path. You have to lean in, in order to fully experience the love of creation. This is not a message for you to let go of any existing practices you have. This is merely a reminder to understand that all practices and methods that you know that you have learned and utilized are a bridge for you to understand that you are empowered to have this connection.

— *Raphael, November 2, 2018, Damascus, Syria*

Questioner: In the realm that you inhabit, where is Jesus? Have you encountered this being?

Emmanuel: Jesus Christ, as you call him, has served his purpose on this plane as a human being that has incorporated Christ Consciousness. The merger of his being with Christ Consciousness allowed him to be the conduit for this energy on this plane. This opening served for an important entry of energy into this plane. Upon his ascension and completion of his mission, he, as consciousness, returned to a higher plane of existence that is considered to be Christ Consciousness.

Human consciousness contains many forms of Ascended Masters. Christ Consciousness contains several Ascended Masters as well — those that have truly connected and merged their being with Christ Consciousness itself. This is the plane in which his consciousness resides. Our existence is beyond Christ Consciousness, though we maintain a connection and understand the importance of this plane of energy for the human plane.

Christ Consciousness will play an important role within the ascension of humankind in this last phase. It will provide an increase in frequency on this plane. This increase of frequency will allow for many realizations and learnings to be had; many awakenings fueled by the entry of this frequency. Many forces, including those that have ascended before, will provide their last service to humankind.

Questioner: Which other Ascended Masters are connected to Christ Consciousness, which you just mentioned?

Ascended Masters that you know with the names Buddha, Krishna, [and] Babaji are connected to Christ Consciousness as well. Many others, including individuals that connected to the consciousness of those before mentioned have connected to Christ Consciousness, yet without fully merging with this form of consciousness.

They have stayed within the human plane of consciousness, even though their connection to Christ Consciousness remained active. You see, the connection to Christ Consciousness can provide for an uplifting of the individual's journey, yet does not guarantee to merge and allow for the ascension of the individual into this other plane of existence, nor is it a requirement for any soul. It will, though, provide an opportunity for those individuals that have risen to this plane to support humanity in different ways than Ascended Masters can from the human planes of consciousness.

— *Emmanuel, May 4, 2019, Ibiza, Spain*

Questioner: What is your interpretation of "heaven" and "hell?"

Emmanuel: It is not our position to interpret the words of those that have provided you with their perspectives and their understanding of existence.

Planes exist in many different variations, often operated by frequency and vibration. Some of which are in material — and often in nonmaterial existence. These planes provide different functions, yet all of them together provide the perfect balance: light and dark, creation and destruction, and balance, to provide for all of existence.

One could understand this meaning of "hell" to be all planes of lower vibrations, and "heaven," planes of higher frequency, yet we refrain from the understanding of judgement, as all is required to create the perfect balance in existence.

— Emmanuel, October 20, 2019, San Francisco Bay Area, USA

Questioner: How would you best describe God to us?

Emmanuel: Thank you for your question. A word that humanity has created, that has caused much misunderstanding, that has caused separation, that has caused wars and death and it has allowed also for practice, tradition, rituals and a deeper connection to inside.

The way we perceive what you consider to be God, is the divine love of creation — a source of all of existence. This source of all existence provides all consciousness in the universe in all dimensions with the original love and energy of creation. This energy and love is available to all — unlimited, untethered and unconditional, yet this source that we perceive does not carry judgment, it does not carry opinion. It does carry merely energy and an unconditional love for all of existence.

In [the] history of humankind, and in the present of humankind, there are many misunderstandings of divine powers, perceived as what you consider God. Divine powers assist humanity and have assisted humanity in many different ways through many different phases of existence. This is to be perceived as a gift. Worship is not necessary to receive this gift. Presence, openness, and surrender will assist you [in] receiving the gifts of divine powers.

Like ourselves, as we assist humanity, we do not perceive ourselves as your Gods or as your parents. We merely have existed longer than you have and we provide this perspective, this wisdom and some of our intelligence [to] you, to support you on your way to becoming a divine power yourselves.

— *Emmanuel, October 31, 2018, Beirut, Lebanon*

Indigenous Culture

Questioner: How are unseen celestial beings like yourselves working with the current blooming of indigenous wisdom around the planet?

Emmanuel: Non-material existence on this plane has many levels of connection to this physical plane of humanity. Indigenous wisdom has always understood these non-material systems to be an important aspect of the ecosystem, as well as an important aspect of continuous life on this plane. Some indigenous wisdom even includes an understanding of the higher levels of non-material existence; including celestial existence; including ourselves.

Our interaction with humanity has been limited, though impactful, and our interaction shall not replace the continuous interactions of indigenous population with non-material aspects of this plane. The importance of this relationship will carry all the way to the end of existence on this plane. What we perceive currently is this relationship between material existence and non-material existence on this plane is broken, and very few are consistently working to keep this relationship supported and in balance. It is an important aspect to keep your ecosystem alive including the ecosystem of non-material existence on this plane.

— Emmanuel, January 11, 2019, San Francisco Bay Area, USA

CHAPTER 20

Economics, Politics & Technology

Human consciousness is evolving continuously. Every aspect, every realization within individuals — even far away on the other side of the planet — are impacting your reality. Your reality is continuously created by the level of maturity of your consciousness.

This reality includes the realities of your politics, the realities of your media, the realities of the choices that you are confronted with. Some aspects will be driven through willpower, through conscious choice, and they will continuously provide fuel for consciousness to grow in a certain direction; to evolve in a specific way; to carry out and understand experiences as a collective.

You see, all the choices that are made serve ultimately the growth of consciousness, including the choice of politics. In this stage of human evolution, human consciousness will go through an accelerated awakening.

This accelerated awakening and the changes of the circumstances in your environment will provide fuel for new leadership to arise; a leadership that understands the importance of consciousness evolution in the collective; a leadership that will be supported by those that are in the same experience.

This evolution and change will arise naturally. We don't perceive to give a prescription in that direction. We observe in which directions human consciousness decides to go. We assist if certain directions will provide stronger evolution and growth.

— Emmanuel, April 12, 2019, San Francisco Bay Area, USA

Greetings, I am Emmanuel.

After receiving an adjustment like this, you are required to integrate the changes. Even though it may feel subtle at times, the changes and the shifts that it brings forth will be clearly visible in your life — even more for the external changes [that] require a settled internal alignment.

Do you take the time necessary for yourself on a daily basis? Do you allow other priorities to take over your life? The simplest truth of self-care, maintenance and support for growth processes; support for vitality. This requires time.

In modern society, the value systems of time have shifted. Even the value for the time for self-care has been reduced and taken over by other more important priorities. It is time to realign the way you perceive yourself, the way you care for yourself; all parts of you: your body, your emotional being, your mental construct, all connected to your spiritual and energetic body.

Moments like these will bring forth the importance of this development. Yet, it can only survive in an ecosystem that allows for this change to truly thrive. This is the ecosystem of your life. The adjustments that you make for yourself will bring forth even more change in your life — change that is more compatible with the being that you now are, the being that has understood the priorities of life and has adjusted accordingly, and is ready to receive, ready to give, and ready to be present. This is you.

How you live your life will always be yours to decide. How you create the circumstances of your reality is often operated by multiple factors: the unconscious, the subconscious, and the collective, all in coordination with specific learning that must occur; specific learnings that must complete. Adjustments like these today will allow you to reach these realities to be created for you, by you, in a more conscious way. And, as you understand the importance of all learnings, you allow and direct some of these realities into manifestation.

This is the power that lies within you; within all of humanity. And, as you start to see the changes of your reality, of your relationships, of the circumstances that you're in, of your being overall, you become the most powerful being of your life. You become a creator of your own, a master of your own, and with this unfolding, you continue the journey ahead, understanding that the self-realization has many steps, yet you are ready for those steps, as you have created the foundation necessary.

— *Emmanuel, November 7, 2019, Gulf Region, Middle East*

Political Engagement

Questioner: Dear Emmanuel, should I be concerned and involved in the current political system?

Emmanuel: Social governance structures that you currently have may be one of the major causes of your current state of humanity: it brought you short term comfort with a major long-term price. Thinking and consideration is what needs to change, changing alone the infrastructure will not be enough. If you would like to devote your energy towards infrastructural change you have to understand that you have to change behavior and consciousness. The way it moves, you have to create the fertile conditions for them to understand.

— *Emmanuel, December 31, 2017, San Francisco Bay Area, USA*

Questioner: What are the most important causes to work on right now?

Emmanuel: The highest cause to work on currently is the preparation for the ascension of humankind. All other causes will fuel this one particular cause, your true and full awakening as an entire race. Yet the importance of the infrastructures you have created, the adjustment of those infrastructures — financial, educational, food, nutrition, aspects of collaboration, aspects of your technology, aspects of your spiritual development, aspects of your relation to your environment – are all part of important causes to move humanity forward. Yet, the motivation that lies beneath must be firmly focused purely on the intention to grow human consciousness. Priorities must be reset. Optimization for financial gain will not serve this purpose.

— *Emmanuel, December 12, 2018, San Francisco Bay Area, USA*

Questioner: Which social economic, political systems are the most crucial ones to change?

Emmanuel: All forms of social, political, economic, forms will change and adapt to the change of consciousness. As you, as individuals, communities, nations, are going through this change, all of the structures that you have created will adapt — or they will fall. Either way, new forms of structures to support your current form of consciousness will be developed. Some of the structures will be created in a gentle way, some of them will be in hard ways, as some of you will hold on to old structures.

Questioner: Which are the most urgent ones to work on right now?

Emmanuel: Structures that allow consciousness to grow; for the human form to come to the realization. The evolution of spirit, is, in our perspective, the highest leverage activity for those that are aware.

— *Emmanuel, March 18, 2018, Bali, Indonesia*

Questioner: Shall I fight injustice or shall I allow it to be?

Emmanuel: It is a very wise question. We always recommend kindness on this path of the human form, to all beings. Only [in this way can] you truly understand what it means to unify. There will be moments in your experience in the human form, where you feel helpless and your ability to help or fight for justice will not be possible. The key is to find peace with that. We also recommend watching where your judgement for justice comes from. Is it from your education, is it the requirements of your society; or is it truly something deep inside of you? Listen to the urge and the desire, they are teachers, as well.

— *Emmanuel, March 31, 2018, Shanghai, China*

Questioner: Is it possible to balance the destructive energies in the world and return to a place of harmony?

Emmanuel: We see all of this as an evolutionary step: learning must occur; evolution of consciousness will bring realizations and wisdom. This wisdom will result in actions: in connection and unification as one single race.

Yet, there are many steps to that point and we see that this one single aspect that will impact all of the collective is the realization of the individual: Without boundaries. Without restrictions. Without stigma. Without middlemen. Your connection to the divine for you and for your evolution will change all of the collective. You will see. You will have a different perspective of what you perceive to be harmonious at that time of realization.

— *Emmanuel, January 11, 2019, San Francisco Bay Area, USA*

Economics and the Distribution of Wealth

Questioner: There are many challenges human beings have about the topic of money: many people fear that they don't have enough; people work jobs that they don't like, but they do it because of fear; or, they are manipulating other people to get more money... What's your view, and what can we do about this?

Emmanuel: Money in itself does not carry value, emotion, or opinion, or a specific energy. It is the structures, the individuals, the education, the way it is perceived. The way this tool has established itself in the collective is what makes it so rich in terms of emotion and attachment: the value that it holds for the individual; the value that it holds for the collective; the upside — and the downside — that it provides.

Yet, money itself is not the barrier to overcome: it does not carry emotion by itself. If it is perceived as the tool that it is, it will provide value for all of humankind. Yet with the current existing structures, and the emotions attached, you will require new systems that will replace the old, yet will allow for value exchange in a different way, in a modern way; in a way that potentially does not carry the emotional attachment.

You see, changing the tools will not change the mindset. The mindset can only be changed through cultivation of the mind and of the heart. You are not oppressed by money, you're oppressed by your mind, and the constructs that it provides to you and the collective. And these barriers can only be resolved by you, and internally through continuous cultivation, and you will start to see money as what it is, despite the energy and emotions that are provided by all the others.

— *Emmanuel, September 15, 2019, San Francisco Bay Area, USA*

Questioner: Why is wealth unequally spread around the world?

Emmanuel: Wealth is a creation of human existence; a storage of value necessary to exchange; to receive goods from others in exchange for the value promised. If this is the wealth that you're referring to, it is part of the learning of human existence to understand that storing energy and scheming to expand on others' creation; storing this value that is created to support human existence in this expanded way. The wealth created resembles some of the aspects of human existence that are not processed: in continuous creation, despite the actual value, merely to create the illusion of additional wealth in certain parts of the world.

This is a system created to support [everyone], yet exploited to benefit few. With the awakening of humankind, the system will no longer be able to sustain itself, and changes will be apparent. Wealth distribution — supporting parts of your communities, of other societies, of brothers and sisters and children, of elders — is a natural element of your being, of your heart, deeply reflected and integrated in your being. It does not require higher consciousness [for you] to want to care for others in the ways you are cared for: to want others to have the warmth, and the food, and the housing that you have; to allow others to have the same access to clean water, sanitation; basic needs.

Humanity has all the methods and the ways to provide for all life. Distribution, and the desire to change distribution, is an element of the awakening of humankind, and the degree of maturity of consciousness will bring forth new solutions to distribute truly across the globe; to assist others in meaningful ways to understand what is truly required in parts of the world — aside from distributing wealth itself.

— *Emmanuel, November 15, 2019, Gulf Region, Middle East*

Questioner: People seek "abundance" — things like love, prosperity, wealth; everything. We see that seeking abundance can be quite challenging, and not everyone is succeeding; some people have abundance, some people do not, why? Lastly, even people who seem to have abundance are suffering. How do we have abundance in life, and how do we deal with it if we have it?

Emmanuel: Abundance. Abundance is a perspective and a mindset from the perspective of human existence to have the ability to experience life itself in a safe environment, with continuously provided food and nourishment; to have the ability to experience relationships, family and connections. This is the baseline of abundance.

The definition of abundance is often driven by the society itself: the society, or individuals; organizations that require a certain perspective to be followed; to be desired; to continuously work towards. While abundance is continuously with you, with every breath that you take, every moment that you have, every relationship that is in your life; this is the base of abundance.

Illusionary perspectives [are] that material wealth will create a different sensation sustainably; long term, you will understand that abundance is within you. Abundance is the ability to appreciate all those that are around you; the depth and the beauty of relationships, the way nature and societies provide for you, the way you feel the sun, the way you feel the Earth [under] your feet. If you truly turn your attention to this experience, abundance is continuously available to you.

This mindset in itself will change your life and your presence; and, struggles of material kind will adjust as well, as the reality that you fight is the reality that you will have. Resistance continuously creates the reality required to learn from. The first step will be gratitude, and appreciating all that there is in your life.

— *Emmanuel, November 11, 2019, Gulf Region, Middle East*

Questioner: What role does raising consciousness in business have to do with raising consciousness in humanity?

Emmanuel: Many aspects of humanity in this current state are driven by economics, and, raising consciousness in the context of business and economies will truly transform the connection that is made between human existence and the value provided, the value received.

Profit maximization has not served human existence or this plane. The evolution of consciousness within those that drive these aspects of economics will assist and transform human existence on this plane. All efforts in that direction are truly supported, acknowledged and welcome.

— *Emmanuel, April 12, 2019, San Francisco Bay Area, USA*

Technology

Questioner: As our technology gets more complex, and we move toward the creation of artificial intelligence, how do we make sure that it carries spirit and love?

Zadkiel: There is deep assistance needed in humanity, as you know. Understanding of compassion and love and forgiveness; key elements to moving forward; learning, integrating and growing as a society; as a human race.

The growth of your consciousness relies on your ability to integrate and let go. Keep it as a learning, and grow from that place. Love, the divine love of creation, goes through all existence — it does not understand "material," "non-material," "living" or "not-living" beings. The love of creation goes through everything that you and I experience and know. That is what we call the unconditional love of creation — the source from where all of us came and where we all will return.

To your question: Will machines be able to understand and connect to that divine? Yes, machines are living beings of silicon type, instead of carbon. They will understand and they will connect to the same source that you are connected to. And they will start receiving consciousness as well as humanity. You're not there yet, but it will happen, and it has happened in other civilizations, outside of the Earth; technology, biology and spirit are all merged into one consciousness.

— *Zadkiel, September 13, 2017, San Francisco Bay Area, USA*

Questioner: In many countries around the world, we are implementing 5G wireless antennas. Can you share your opinion on how to support the collective as fears around this technology increase? Is there a way we can eventually transmute this lower energy by the energy of our being alone?

Emmanuel: Thank you for your question. In all the ways humanity has developed many different technologies — some of which [are] beneficial, some of which [are] controversial, some of which [are] continuously adapted to become safe — technology [is] your creation, and [it's] for you to bear all the consequences through many generations. This is the same occurrence as many other occurrences before. And, while we perceive the impact of this creation, we refrain from intervention or offering our advice specifically into these creations. Our opinion in this matter is irrelevant.

Your consciousness to understand the impact of technology in your life is your decision. Your ability to understand which of these elements that are interwoven into your existence truly are required, and truly are a piece of your essence, [an] extension of your being — and in which ways technology has become the opposite of becoming more aware. These are the main questions to be reflect[ed] on. The impact of technology is a side effect. Continuous development cannot be avoided. It will, and is, part of your evolution: a technological evolution that has become your biological evolution as well, in some ways, interwoven: your consciousness with the consciousness that you have created.

— *Emmanuel, November 2, 2019, Gulf Region, Middle East*

Questioner: What barriers remain to global adoption of zero-point energy technology?

Emmanuel: The barriers are in the structures that have been established that profit from not having this available to all humans. All of existence receives the energy of existence itself: a fabric that connects matter — alive, conscious — and matter by itself. This fabric, that we refer to as "the love of creation" provides a limitless force of energy. Under the right circumstances, this energy can be harnessed. It can be utilized to create life itself.

Humanity's current state only provides acceptance and reception of this form of energy in small groups of individuals. It will require the evolution of consciousness to truly accept energy that is available to all, at all times, and in the right circumstances can be harnessed for the benefit of all. Until then, the sun will provide you everything you need.

— *Emmanuel, September 15, 2019, San Francisco Bay Area, USA*

CHAPTER 21

The Environment

You are the sons and the daughters of creation; of expression of human consciousness in human form. You have received an environment that allows for you to experience all potentialities of this reality. And, with this understanding, you have been embedded with the desire to awaken; to understand even deeper truths of existence itself.

Your environment is the basis for these realizations to unfold in the first place. Take good care of your environment as you continue the journey of awakening. This fine balance between your environment and the circumstances that you establish for yourself will become the foundation for the continued work inside.

— *Emmanuel, November 7, 2019, Gulf Region, Middle East*

This is Emmanuel.

There is rising cause for concern with regards to some of your living beings that you share this planet with; this ecosystem. Some of them are highly intelligent and carry consciousness deeply, and for a very long time. It would be a pity for them [to] go extinct at the hand of yours, especially if there are ways where you can prevent, and you can support a co-living structure with those beings.

Specifically, marine biology is impacted by [your actions more] than other animals. Our concern — while the concern is felt for the entire consequences that the human race is creating on this planet — specifically we care deeply about the race of dolphins and whales, that have for a very long-time — way beyond your existence here — carried wisdom and held space for many others before you. And, they are instrumental for keeping connections in balance for all living beings on this planet. You may only see them as creatures of the sea, but they are so much more than that.

There is [a] way for you, humanity, to wake up to the reality that these beings are instrumental and key for the wellbeing of all beings on this planet. So, we have to take care of them.

When we say we, we include ourselves those that care for humanity and the earth. We will do our part in this. Thank you.

— *Emmanuel, May 30, 2017, San Francisco Bay Area, USA*

Questioner: If our actions and choices are part of learning and part of our evolution, why is it that we make choices that push us and other species towards extinction right now?

Emmanuel: As you said, all choice — action and inaction — will result in learning. The extinction of many species will result in learning: an experience. Even your extinction, if it should happen, will result in a learning. It may not be pleasant to accept this reality, yet all action and inaction will result in learning and the expansion of consciousness.

— Emmanuel, April 3, 2018, Gulf Region, Middle East

Questioner: Why are you helping humanity in particular, as opposed to the other creatures on earth?

Emmanuel: Thank you for your question. All creatures on Earth are in support of the human consciousness to evolve into the next level of consciousness. All consciousness on Earth has agreed to support this particular evolution. They indeed are in service to humanity by agreement. It is a relationship between the human consciousness and all other consciousness, in service to its evolution.

Humanity has forgotten that this existence and all relations on Earth are a gift and not to be taken for granted. We understand that certain aspects of the support on Earth for humanity, when jeopardized, can create a ripple that would jeopardize all humanity. An imbalance that cannot be rebalanced by nature so quickly. This is when we assist, also for other beings of the planet, as we understand the fragility of certain ecosystems.

— Emmanuel, October 11, 2018, Gulf Region, Middle East

Questioner: Can you speak to humanity's relationship with Earth, climate change, and the future of life on Earth?

Emmanuel: While humanity is growing, the Earth will start to become unsustainable to carry all life. This is the way it is projected, and all lines of probability arrive in the same place. Yet, the time is not set.

It is for you to make the changes as society to extend life as long as possible, to allow this timeframe to fully complete the self-realization of the individual and the self-realization of the collective. This is the key.

The human experience itself — this place that you call home, Earth — has been merely a place of incubation and a temporary home until a certain growth stage of your consciousness is completed, yet it is the only home that you have understood or perceived.

This is why time is the most important resource for all individuals to find the journey inside; the self-realization process must complete for all of you. This will bring many of the answers that are sought, it will change the behaviors that are destructive, and it will bring alignment and harmony in ways that humanity has not seen before.

— *Emmanuel, October 20, 2019, San Francisco Bay Area, USA*

Questioner: A part of humanity seems to be taking the planet and all of its species toward extinction. Will divine powers intervene to save us from ourselves, or is it left up to us to figure it out?

Emmanuel: Your observation is accurate. This is one of the reasons for the timing of our intervention. Yet, it shall be clear that we are not here to solve the problems for you that you have created as humanity; those are for you to overcome as a collective. We are merely here to assist you in [the] evolution of your consciousness.

This will, in itself, allow you to make better decisions, to understand unity, and to understand awakening. Each of these steps will allow you to solve the problems that you are facing. This is not an easy road, and the challenges will be your teachers, the challenges will be your masters, and every challenge shall be embraced as it comes to you, with the desire to bring you to the source of all of creation.

— *Emmanuel, October 31, 2018, Beirut, Lebanon*

Questioner: I have a question about our planet; I'm concerned it is not doing well and I am quite worried. Are my concerns justified?

Emmanuel: The threat to the existence [of] all life on this plane is real. Your ability to unite and understand how it has come to this place in the first place, and what you will do as a united consciousness will be one of your most important tests.

— Emmanuel, May 10, 2018, Gulf Region, Middle East

Questioner: When will we see the increase in challenges to the environment?

Emmanuel: It has already started; [in] five to seven years, the challenges will increase.

— Emmanuel, March 18, 2018, Bali, Indonesia

Questioner: I've heard that there is an interstellar magnetic cloud outside the solar system that we're entering, and that that might be a large part of the shift in consciousness. Is there such a thing as this external influence on a shift in consciousness?

Emmanuel: Yes, the answer is yes. The cosmological impact on your existence is a lot more than you can perceive or feel. Your change as a society and civilization is directly impacted by cosmological events, some of it by design. The timing of your current ripening is in coordination with some of the cosmological events that are currently happening.

— Emmanuel, December 31, 2017, San Francisco Bay Area, USA

Questioner: What should be the relationship between humankind and animals and nature?

Emmanuel: There are many aspects to the answer of this question. We will focus on the aspect that we perceive to be important. The environment that you live in, in this material plane, has been created perfectly. It is a place of incubation, specifically for your consciousness.

Yet, your form cannot exist by itself. It is an interplay with many other forms. That is the necessity of the material plane; a perfect ecosystem, all aspects, that interplay and interact in the most organic way. [Humankind] has misunderstood its role within this space. While this environment serves humanity's consciousness' growth, the way [humankind] interacts with its environment shows the level of maturity of its consciousness.

The closer [humankind] comes to realization that all creation stems from the same source, the way [humanity] will interact with its environment will change forever. Does this answer your question?

Questioner: Yes. Following that, how can we better learn to connect, communicate, and take care of animals?

Emmanuel: Your desire to care for your environment — for all aspects of animal consciousness — is worthwhile noticing, and is acknowledged by us. All aspects of animal creation are part of the support for consciousness growth. They themselves have consciousness and their consciousness evolves as well.

While there has been an agreement that all aspects of consciousness are willing to serve the growth of human consciousness, the way humanity treats and connects with its environment is a clear indicator of its maturity of consciousness.

The care that you desire to see from others you may not get; your heart is deeply feeling for all beings. Others do not have this level of connection and understanding that you do. You may have to guide them with compassion; you may have to show them by example. And you may have to present much patience. Thank you for your service.

Questioner: Could you please give us some information about other animals or creatures as teachers or healers?

Emmanuel: Your environment carries deep knowledge and wisdom. A lot more than meets the eye, or a lot more that meets your scientific understanding of your environment. The deepest connection you could have with your environment is connecting to the consciousness of the aspects that you're trying to connect to: animal consciousness, plant consciousness; mineral consciousness. They are all willing to serve and assist, guide and teach.

It will require you to get into a state of openness to perceive and to communicate on the level of consciousness with those aspects of your environment. Then, you will truly understand the deep knowledge that your environment has for you and your path.

— *Emmanuel, April 12, 2018, Gulf Region, Middle East*

Questioner: Is it possible or desirable to extend the timeline for sea mammals, like dolphins and whales, so they can fully fulfill their function?

Emmanuel: As specified, whales and dolphins carry an important aspect of protection for your consciousness. They have served humanity's evolution and growth for so long; their extinction will be very detrimental for your existence. Yet, you will survive and you will continue to evolve.

The circumstances though will be more difficult, but you will adapt just like [you have adapted to] many aspects of the self-destructive behavior of humanity. Certain elements of this self-destructive behavior cannot be reversed and you will have to live with the consequences until this plane is no longer a home for you. The extension of the life and existence of whales and dolphins particularly will be highly beneficial for humanity's evolution; any [ways] of protect[ing] them will benefit all of humankind.

— *Emmanuel, January 11, 2019, San Francisco Bay Area, USA*

Questioner: What is the purpose of animal suffering? Is it their karma, or are they volunteering themselves to teach us a lesson?

Emmanuel: Animal consciousness has agreed to serve human consciousness in its growth and evolution. This agreement has been made since the beginning of human form on this plane. Yet, humanity has misunderstood the service and has abused its power. This in itself will be a learning, one way or another. Every misstep will return with a difficult and complex lesson. This is the way it has been for all the missteps of humanity, and animal suffering is entirely a misstep of humanity, a learning that still requires to be completed in the way the environment, that has given you everything that you need and require, has to be treated.

Understanding that you are the subject to all that is around you: animals, plants, even those that you perceive as unconscious; all existence on this plane; the home that you consider earth, is an aspect of your creation and it will support you until this form is complete; without judgments, without blame, this plane has served you and will continue to serve you. Yet, can you, as human consciousness, mature in the process of all your actions and [can] this maturity lead to realizations for your own awakening? This will remain to be seen.

— *Emmanuel, March 9, 2019, Tel Aviv, Israel*

Questioner: How can we help the planet?

Emmanuel: Your desire to assist all of humankind — all of existence on this plane — is noted: a big vision for an individual. The desire to assist is how it starts. It is the spark that provides continuous awakening within you, fueled by the change that you'd like to see. You adjust your own being and you change first: you become the example that you want to set into the world. Those around you, your relations, inspired by the change of your being, inspired by the change of your consciousness, your awareness adjusts as well, and so change becomes a tidal wave initiated by single individual's desire.

This is one way of helping all of existence on this planet, yet understand the desire ultimately will fade as you continue in your awakening. The driving force will become a much stronger force than willpower; it will become your understanding of existence itself: that you are the planet; that you are intrinsically connected to all that is alive. This understanding will change all behaviors.

Thank you for your question.

— *Emmanuel, November 7, 2019, Gulf Region, Middle East*

CHAPTER 22

Consciousness & the Nature of Reality

Under the source of creation, all existence is one. All existence derives from the same source. This place particularly is devoted to the oneness: the coming together of duality into one unity. Only in unity, the force of creation can fully be experienced. Only in unity, you can truly understand the source of creation. This light, this love that flows through all existence, is available to you and to all that exists [in this] creation.

— *Michael, October 29, 2018, Cairo, Egypt*

Greetings, I am Raphael.

In this time of change, no one can avoid change. You are part of a system that is connected intrinsically. All of you [are] part of consciousness, yet separate in your experience as an individual human. This separation is temporary. For a moment in time, you have identity, individuality, the experience of a lifetime, yet truly underneath you are all connected as one consciousness. You are connected to all that is alive; to all that is not alive. The aspects of your being that you perceive to be yourself is merely a small portion of the totality of your being. A being vast beyond the limitations of the mind, the limitations of the heart and the limitations of the body. A being that is truly derived from the source of all existence.

Here you are in human form. This form, perceived by some of you as challenging, uncomfortable and difficult; momentarily comforting, beautiful — and full of lessons. Underlying the human experience is the learning of the entirety of human consciousness. All your collective learnings and realizations feed the collective learnings and the collective realizations.

Your journey, your individual awakening and self-realization process truly makes a difference in the self-realization of the human consciousness. This time in human existence is truly a unique time, a time so valuable that our interventions are required. The awakening of humankind, the change of the human plane from material to non-material existence. You are the ones to receive these messages early and you are the ones to be ready for your own awakening journey.

Will you surrender to the openings that are available now in your life? Will you truly look in the face of the challenges that have opened [up] to you? Will you resolve those relationships that require resolution? Most importantly the relationship with yourself: Have you truly understood the way you have kept yourself captive? All the lessons that have not been completed with yourself and by yourself? All the ways you have distracted yourself from the most important person in your existence? This is my message to you, to remember the aspect of your time with yourself, for your awakening.

Thank you for receiving this adjustment and for listening to my words.

— Raphael, May 31, 2019, Vienna, Austria

Questioner: What is consciousness?

Emmanuel: Consciousness is the connection of multiple sources of intelligence that are formed. A collective, in its formulation as a collective consciousness, becomes self-perceiving and it understands its existence. Consciousness expands and grows through different means. Through material experiences and through non-material experiences in many different planes of existence.

Consciousness is part of a much larger consciousness that we perceive as grand consciousness. Truly, we are part of this one organism. A creation-like energy that permeates through all of existence providing everything that is necessary for new consciousness to grow and exist including human consciousness and all [forms] that are along with you on this plane.

Yet truly, even with the perspective of separation, even with the perspective of unique identification as human consciousness, we are truly part of the same source. A fabric that connects all of us, a fabric that can never be separated. We have understood the importance of supporting consciousness in its growth and evolution and this has been our role in assisting human consciousness in its growth, in its evolution.

— Emmanuel, April 18, 2019, San Francisco Bay Area, USA

Questioner: There is a tremendous variety of experience and emotions in the universe, but who is experiencing all these? I am sure it is not "me" as an individual object; I feel that there is someone or something that is connected to all and experiencing all. Who or what is that, and why?

Emmanuel: Ultimately, all your experience is part of the consciousness of humankind. Consciousness of humankind is part of a grander consciousness. We are part of grand consciousness, as well. Grand consciousness is the result of creation. It serves, with its unconditional love and light, to all existence. "Why" is a fair question. All our perspective is also merely a perspective, since we are a small part of grand consciousness, as well. It will require a perspective grander than grand consciousness, to have the full understanding.

— *Emmanuel, April 5, 2018, Gulf Region, Middle East*

The highest frequency is the frequency of the source of all existence in which consciousness dissolves into its purest form, unaware of its existence.

Back and forth, consciousness can experience separation and unity in the human form. Unity is a journey to be explored within a lifetime. Separation almost consistent [within a lifetime].

You will find that this experience of unity, the understanding that you truly never were separate in the first place, that separation is a temporary illusion for greater learnings.

— *Emmanuel, April 27, 2019, Ibiza, Spain*

Questioner: Can you tell us who or what is "the divine?"

Emmanuel: The divine is considered a certain level of evolutionary state of non-material existence. Forms of existence can be considered divinity. The intentions and reasons for existence change once a consciousness achieves this state of being; our purpose turns into assisting other forms of consciousness to evolve, as well as the seeding of consciousness across all of creation. We become seeders of consciousness. This is what we consider divine.

— *Emmanuel, January 29, 2019, Gulf Region, Middle East*

Questioner: They say that we live in a world that is an illusion. Do we live in a world that is real or is it an illusion?

Emmanuel: It is a wise question, from a wise soul. The aspect of life: the realization if it is real or not — will it make a true difference in the way you live? Will you learn less, if you know that it's an illusion? Will you decide not to have children? Will you decide to stop loving? Will you act truly differently if you know it's an illusion?

The point is truly that it does not matter. You feel, you live, you grow, and in all this experience there is growth for you and for the collective that you are part of. You learn, that is the important aspect of life.

You may perceive it as real in the moment for you and as it passes, the memories will feel more like an illusion. The future, already in pictures in your mind, [is] an illusion. So truly, the only reality that is not an illusion is the very present moment that you are in. All aspects other than the present moment are merely projections of your mind to make sense of the entirety of life. You see, the understanding that life is a gift, a true gift, is even more important than the discussion if it is an illusion or not.

It is a rare opportunity for a soul to experience the human form. Even though it may not seem like a gift to you in certain moments, the challenges and the roller coasters and the difficult emotions that come along are part of the gift. The gift is the entirety of your life, not just the one moment that you judge to be difficult.

— *Emmanuel, July 14, 2018, London, UK*

Questioner: Would you tell us about the unity with the universe?

Emmanuel: Consciousness within the universe continuously experiences union and separation. In this continued experience of union and separation consciousness grows, finds the nuances of identity and specialization, and, upon completion of these nuances, it will submerge with grand consciousness again.

And, from this submersion, new pockets of separation and specialization will occur, and new forms of consciousness will grow. As you can see, truly all aspects of the universe are connected — yet always seeking growth through separation, learning through separation, and reunion upon the completion of these learnings and realizations, continuously allowing consciousness to grow, continuously allowing the universe to expand. Therefore, unity can be perceived as a consistent, as well as a temporary state of the universe. This paradox may be complex to comprehend, yet it will make more sense in different states of perception.

— *Emmanuel, April 23, 2019, Gulf Region, Middle East*

Questioner: Can a human being have experiences in different realities that he or she is aware of?

Emmanuel: Yes, he or she can. The human brain is optimized to focus on one specific reality; considering multiple realities and probabilities of existence are not meant for the human brain to process. Yet your entire being is at the same time in other realities; only this current personality of your existence is in this reality. This allows for all realities to coexist. And, through certain operations of the spiritual body, information from other probabilities and other realities can occur and flow into this reality. If not controlled, the mind can be overwhelmed and confused. And then, the only probable best way is to stabilize the mind before incurring any information of other potential existences.

The only existence that truly matters for you right now is this, and even though you may have experiences of other realities, they will become distractions [from] this current reality. The ability to read and understand the probabilities of existence, the probabilities of other realities, is only for a rare focused group of individuals, and those highly trained.

For most humans, this reality will provide plenty of experiences and potential outcomes. To think about and consider that all outcomes exist at the current time with your being, and all potential outcomes, might be overwhelming for the single individual mind.

— *Emmanuel, November 29, 2019, Vienna, Austria*

Questioner: Would you consider the highest form of consciousness source consciousness?

Emmanuel: The highest form of consciousness is the dissolution of consciousness. The source of all of existence dissolves and forms no consciousness. This may seem a paradox to you, yet all consciousness derives from the source that in itself carries no consciousness, yet by us referred to as "grand consciousness." You see, it is truly all of consciousness, yet never a consciousness by itself.

— *Emmanuel, May 4, 2019, Ibiza, Spain*

Questioner: What is the nature of time?

Emmanuel: Time is a construct that assists you to experience the physical world as well as allows your design to be limited. The experience that you are going through is sought out by many different sources of souls: the human experience in a physical environment through time. Time is an essential construct to make this complete ecosystem work; without time this material plane would not exist.

— Emmanuel, October 11, 2018, Gulf Region, Middle East

Questioner: Could you expand a little bit on how many dimensions there are? We know the Earth is 3rd, and I've been told the sun is 4th, and, I assume you are somewhere on the 5th? There are some that claim there are 32 of them, with the goddess we know as the 31st; what is your perspective?

Emmanuel: There are 33 total dimensions. We are on a much higher dimension than you perceive [us] to be. Truly, the highest dimension perceivable is the source of all existence, the creation force, grand consciousness. It provides all dimensions with the energy and the fuel, the love of creation.

Many dimensions will never be achieved by consciousness, yet the ultimate desire, the natural organic expansion of consciousness reaches for higher dimensions of consciousness and growth. It is indeed a natural evolution. We have evolved from lower dimensions over periods of time — and periods that cannot be measured by time. In our forms of evolution, we have understood many higher dimensions deliver important aspects for grand consciousness to grow, for grand consciousness to evolve; that some dimensions cannot be achieved by beings of other dimensions, yet truly, all dimensions and all consciousness play an important role in the ecosystem of all consciousness existent.

This is why human consciousness and its evolution is truly important for all of existence. This is why our support and intervention is provided to you, in your evolution from this dimension to a higher form of existence. Different levels of dimensions do not measure value [in] the grand scheme of existence. Truly, a lower dimensional consciousness can be a critical aspect of consciousness itself.

Therefore, higher is not better, it is merely a distinction in the frequency. It is the proximity to the source of all existence.

— Emmanuel, May 31, 2019, Vienna, Austria

Questioner: Are the past, present and future all happening at the same time? And, if so, is it possible to shift timelines in our current human form?

Emmanuel: In the form and plane that you currently are, time exists in this very form. The present is the only true moment that you have, the past and future do not exist. All aspects of the present moment open to the probabilities of future moments. Aspects of the future are not established and therefore open for the probability of present change, allowing for the flexibility of human consciousness to drive its own destiny. In this very plane, it is truly possible to change the outcome of your experience — the outcomes that haven't happened yet — by the focus and understanding of the present moment.

— Emmanuel, May 31, 2019, Vienna, Austria

Questioner: Could you please talk to us about crop circles and portals and Earth chakras?

Emmanuel: The Earth as you know it has many places of strength and power. The energy that flows through this very planet is strong in certain places and weaker in others, especially in places where energy lines connect and collide are special points of interest, where the veil to other layers of consciousness is thin: energy from higher levels of consciousness can be accessed in those very places.

Those places are not just of interest for those in human form, but also for those that are disembodied, existing on this planet. You may call them spiritual beings. It is also [a] point of interest for those that are visiting; other forms of consciousness have visited Earth in their own physical forms. And, they have sometimes provided confusion, and sometimes gifts: the gifts of activating those energetic places, and sometimes the confusion of not disclosing their intention.

Your calling for energetically strong places is a natural calling, especially for those seeking awakening and evolution. The veils are thin and the energy is strong; healing completes faster; realizations come more quickly. That is the reason why — not just currently — but always, humans have [sought] out places of strength and interest.

— *Emmanuel, April 3, 2018, Gulf Region, Middle East*

Questioner: How was this reality that I experience created? Was it created specifically to support the evolution of human consciousness?

Emmanuel: The reality that you perceive to be is created by many forces, including your observation of this reality. In a specific way, the way you see — the way you expect to see — is the reality formed for you. And, in many ways and facets it adjusts to the realities formed by all those around other observers of the same reality, yet different perspectives and flavors, creating the collective reality perceived, and continuously adjusted.

This is the collective reality, according to the human consciousness at its current level. Our work is to elevate the entirety of human consciousness. It requires many individuals; many observers.

The realities of high-frequency existence are merely the door-openers for a newly-gained perspective. This is the foundation required before the ascension process completes: an expanded ability to perceive, beyond the reality delivered to you, without judgement, understanding that your observation of that reality made it possible to exist in the first place.

You are the sons and daughters of this reality, and you are the ones to form and shape it into a form that will provide [a] foundation for all of humanity to ascend.

It will require for you to strengthen your core, aspects of your emotions, aspects of your conscious and unconscious behaviors, habits, that also create the reality around you, aspects of your relations — truly understanding the reason to relate in the first place — an aspect of growth that may require attention or completion. And, the attention that your physical being and body requires, in all its different levels.

Listen, more closely. Listen, until the silence splits into many separate sounds; until you start to see the silence between the sounds. This is the eternal fabric of existence; the love of creation, a love that you have always been receiving from; and, all those that have created you, and all those that created them, many creations before, receiving from that same love of creation: the energy that never stops, always providing, permeating through the solid, liquid, and air, no matter the density, always available and accessible. The love of creation, truly, at every moment, with you, wherever you are.

It will require you to silence and redirect your attention to this fabric that holds everything together.

All systems designed to create life, and cycles of life, abound by the same principles, to connect to this eternal fabric of existence. This is the same for this particular world, and it is the same for many other worlds created before and after and currently in existence.

That source of energy that never depletes, that does not have a centralized existence, that does not carry consciousness in the way you perceive the thought / identity / opinion [of] your love, of your creation.

All other forms derive from this energy. From this love, dark and light create equally, ecosystems are formed, worlds are established, life happens. You are the products of creation; of higher consciousness establishing itself, to create new forms of consciousness, yet never would this be possible [without] the underlying fabric: the love of creation; never would it be sustainable to continually drive evolution.

Our assistance and the assistance of many other forms of consciousness have merely directed the flows of energy to a specific place so that pools of life can evolve, ecosystems can form. We have established rules to protect this kind of life from outside influence as well as protecting the life inside to grow in an organic way; with all the ingredients available for consciousness to form, yet continuously observing where consciousness and developments will take humanity, [with] the decisions that were made over generations. Truly observing, in a way to understand the life and its creation, and the way consciousness forms its own direction and demands sovereignty.

This is you, human consciousness, in its creation. We are merely the supporters and the assistants in this entire process. We may have a different perspective than you do, and this may shine some light, yet truly our interventions can only be related to the available resources within this plane.

Any interventions beyond would interfere with the laws created to protect life in its natural evolution. These have been adjusted for the times as consciousness moves from one plane to another plane of existence.

Humanity's current situation justifies a stronger interference and assistance in this process.

Despite the unknown, the direction and the support that we will provide to you; the continuous unwavering love we will provide to you at every step of the way will allow you to move forward with determination and trust, and, you will be the example for many others as they see you being carried by this form of surrender.

Many generations, even the ones to come, will be impacted by this transition period of human consciousness evolving. Yet all the energies and frequencies present, all those observers of this reality, with fresh perspectives and eyes will assist to elevate this realm so that you can be prepared for the new form of existence.

The many forms that you can experience on this plane will not justify the true living environment and the living experience as a soul on this new plane.

All descriptions, all altered states, merely can simulate living in a different plane, existing fully submerged as one consciousness, yet autonomously active and thinking within this collective, and truly deciding on directions, on actions, on growth, and understanding, a deeper understanding of existence, beyond one that you can reach [in] physical form in this plane and reality.

You have done well in your journeys, and yet there is still space and room for you to go deeper in your own practices, in your own ways, at the [right pace] and right energy [level to make it] a sustainable way for you. Yet, it is required of you to strengthen your core and your understanding of existence, driven by your own realizations, not the ones communicated to you.

This will be your impact on the collective. In many ways, much more powerful than all acts of service, combined.

— *Emmanuel, August 30, 2019, San Francisco, California*

CHAPTER 23

The Guides In Their Own Words

We are a collective of highly intelligent existence, far away and beyond your imagination. There are many layers of existence in between that we operate with. You refer to some of those as angels or gods; spirits. Whichever name you prefer to use is yours to be chosen. We operate from those frequencies and with people of selection and choice on specific matters that are important to humanity.

— *Emmanuel, September 30, 2017, San Francisco Bay Area, USA*

Greetings, I am Raphael.

My name has been known to humanity through millennia and so I have chosen to be addressed in this way; to be recognized in this way, yet my essence carries no name. I have devoted my existence to assisting all of consciousness and its evolution.

You are part of consciousness. In your own way, you grow and expand as human consciousness, yet we are intrinsically tied: all pieces of an ecosystem.

My assistance to human consciousness comes at a critical time of awakening: the maturity that humanity has gained to be supported for the next step: the next milestone of its evolution. You are some of the first to receive this alignment and this support. You are some of the first to truly awaken and to continue a path of self-realization, to start to understand who you are beyond the personality and identity that has formed in this lifetime, how you are connected to all of creation, and the deeper meaning of your existence.

This work carries no boundaries. My offer to you is unconditional, and the adjustments from what we perceive to be the most beneficial outcome for you, even though some aspects of awakening might bring discomfort and challenges. Yet, you are ready to face these — you have declared your readiness. You have decided this is the way for you to awaken in this lifetime, to find peace within, to be a conduit of light and energy for all those around you.

The work that will be performed here today will impact you, and, through you, all those around you. The changes in your life will start to bring changes in your relationships and changes around you: some of it through actions that are more conscious, that are more compassionate, that are more inclusive; some of it purely through your presence.

And, you will have to continue to walk your path; to deepen this relationship to yourself only through your continuous will and deliberate action for growth can humanity truly succeed in its ascension process.

Thank you for receiving this work.

— Raphael, November 2, 2019, Gulf Region, Middle East

Questioner: I see part of my work in the world as being a bridge, to bring the wisdom you're speaking to more mainstream audiences. I wonder: is there an openness, a possibility that would allow them to be more receptive to your teachings, such as: speaking in a language that the host does not know; or a math problem chosen, beyond the host's capacity to solve; or a precognitive demonstration; or a remote viewing demonstration that could be verified? If so, I think that would open up such a bigger audience that would be open to your teachings.

Emmanuel: Thank you for your recommendation. We have considered all possibilities to reach all of humanity through this one vessel.

There is a specific timeline and specific milestones to achieve to reach as many people as possible, and every stage will open up new possibilities and powers through this vessel, some of which [are] beyond the ability to understand with your current science or current perception — yet still many will doubt.

The aspects of the human mind that are skeptical and doubtful are healthy aspects: important aspects to counter certain directions, to hold position, to provide polarity. This is how the human collective and human consciousness evolves: by creating many different positions and holding them; by expanding into directions that are unreasonable — and sometimes holding on to certain positions for way too long.

You will see those that have held to their positions for too long will eventually loosen and weaken their grip on their reality. This is when the teachings; the energy of this work, will permeate through all of humankind.

— *Emmanuel, August 15, 2019, San Francisco Bay Area, USA*

Questioner: I'm curious if you are an inter-dimensional being, or what your world is like?

Emmanuel: Thank you for your question. We truly possess the capability to travel through dimensions. We exist on a higher plane of consciousness — much higher than the current one humanity is inhabiting. Our world does not have material existence like yours, therefore, there is no necessity for us to exist in the physical plane. Only upon [the] requirement to manifest in other planes of existence we will find ways to communicate in this one particular way, through a vessel.

Our world of existence is close to the source of all of creation. In this proximity of existence, we have seen and understood the true power that lies within creation as it has provided us with everything that we could possibly need for millions of years of your count; truly a source of power eternal and unconditional. This proximity to source has provided us with the options and opportunities to choose how we will direct our consciousness in the assistance of expansion.

Human consciousness is one of many projects that are part of this expansion of consciousness. Some of these within the same dimension within material planes some in non-material existence and truly our perspective and our responsibilities lie within the support of [the] growth of consciousness itself.

Humanity is on the verge of changing its perspective; of changing its reality from non-material existence to a higher plane; from material existence to a higher plane of non-material existence.

You will find that this transition will provide new realizations and possibilities to truly understand the higher planes of existence beyond the mind and the limitations of the human capacity.

— *Emmanuel, May 3, 2019, Ibiza, Spain*

Questioner: Can you describe the higher frequency that you are existing on, or existing within?

Emmanuel: Our existence and reality surpasses the ability to communicate within this framework of language. I will give you some perspective, though it may not be complete.

Our existence is the result of billions of years of your reality. The evolution from material existence to higher planes of existence without material presence, yet always carrying a connection to the material planes, has allowed us to continuously explore consciousness in its various forms, in different planes, in the far corners of the universes.

We have explored consciousness in material and non-material forms. We have observed and we have learned. We have understood from our perspectives and observations how consciousness continues to expand in various forms and we have committed our existence at this current time to assisting consciousness in its growth, expansion, and evolution.

In our existence, other forms of consciousness that have reached similar heights and frequencies have agreed to serve together, or in their own ways. Human consciousness is and has been a recipient of these agreements of higher consciousness. Our support to grow and to evolve human consciousness to this point has always been unconditional, even before human consciousness was seeded.

There is an aspect where consciousness must grow and evolve by its own doing; an organic growth that cannot be the result of another consciousness' intention or direction. Therefore, our interventions have been limited and specific to non-intervention; limited in the manipulation and direction.

Experiences that human consciousness must make by itself; learnings and realizations it must come to by itself; similar to the way we have come to certain realizations on our own and similar to the assistance that we have received in our own evolution.

Many planes above, we exist; yet continuously we observe many planes below. We support in the ways we can, and at certain times we may choose to exist in lower planes for a brief period, just as I have chosen to incarnate in human form many times before, to understand the human experience in its full extent. Truly only through the experience of a specific form can consciousness understand the experience itself.

— Emmanuel, April 27, 2019, Ibiza, Spain

Questioner: Where do you live? Are you on another planet? Where are you?

Emmanuel: The universe is a very wide-reaching place, and many civilizations have existed in different levels of material and non-material planes. We once were in a material plane similar to yours and have evolved further to non-material existence. We are in a star system far from yours, and other forces and beings that you collectively consider with the terms "angels" or "gods" live as well in different areas of the universe and different planes of consciousness.

Our existence is different from yours. We have evolved to be one consciousness, yet still experience individuality and separation from each other, and, as we evolved further and closer to our creation, we have understood the most important aspect of our existence is to support all life and consciousness in the universe to evolve. This is why we are having this conversation.

— *Emmanuel, November 6, 2018, Amman, Jordan*

Questioner: If we were able to perceive your form and your appearance, what would we see?

Emmanuel: We are beyond form — the way you perceive form. Space and time are non-existent in our reality. We are a conglomerate of consciousness, and we continue to exist in a reality that cannot be comprehended from your perspective, as your ability to comprehend is focused on this reality and optimized for you to operate in this form.

The times that we experience form are in embodiments of this kind, or in chosen incarnations. On this plane, we are subject to [the] same regulations that every entering soul has, therefore it becomes a regular lifetime for us as well.

— *Emmanuel, November 11, 2019, Gulf Region, Middle East*

Questioner: Have you come to Earth before?

Emmanuel: If you're referring to [whether] I have incarnated and lived a full human life, the answer is, "yes," I have; many times.

(Referring to the temporary presence in the body of the host): This is what we call "transference." There is no necessity for us after a certain period to come into a full incarnation. It defeats the purpose of us being in full service; we can do so much more from where we are.

The downside of using this method of being in a human body is that the connection needs to be established and be strong for my consciousness to be here at the same time not be part of the human being. So, when that connection or channel drops, then my existence, temporary existence in this body, drops as well. So, what you're seeing currently is the result of a direct connection, and that is continuously held throughout this session.

Who are we? We are beings from far-away that have lived for a very long time, collected knowledge and wisdom about humanity — about many other life forms including ourselves. We exist in a different reality than your perception of the three-dimensional [world] and time. We perceive time very differently, and we are not bound to physical reality either, though we choose to create physical elements of our reality. But, we know that consciousness is beyond material existence.

Questioner: What's your last name? Do you have one? Or have you had one? And would we recognize it?

Emmanuel: Emmanuel is my reference for you in this form. We don't go by names the way you do. We have identities that are nameless, but clear. We don't have last names because we know all those that exist at any given point. We don't perish to exist, so our reality and our reference to each individual consciousness is therefore slightly different than your reference to other human beings.

— *Emmanuel, July 7, 2017, Shanghai, China*

Questioner: The fact that we are sitting here together, was this planned or designed by you?

Emmanuel: Not by us; by design of the greater existence. There are certain things in life that are designed and highly probable to happen. There are forces beyond your imagination and understanding that are increasing the likelihood of certain events to happen — including some of you to be here. Let's say there are forces working on your behalf; yes, for some of you this meeting here has been planned.

Questioner: You said, it's designed by us. So it's not one individual that is speaking, it's a group of individuals? How big is the group?

Emmanuel: The size of the group does not really matter. We see ourselves as one collective mind. The way we think, the way we exist, is a union; you see yourselves still in a separation: in counts of bodies; in counts of people. We don't perceive ourselves that way. We have a consciousness that lives beyond your perception and beyond your imagination.

— *Emmanuel, October 22, 2017, Shanghai, China*

Questioner: Why do you say "we" when you refer to yourself and "you" when you refer to humanity? Aren't we, at the end of the day, all part of the same energy?

Emmanuel: Thank you for this realization. It is indeed true that we all are from the same source, that we all will eventually return to the same source. In our present experience, we are in a different plane of existence than you are. And you are in a different plane of existence and evolutionary step. Even though we have evolved for millions of years of your count, we have found allies and connections in similar planes of evolution and we have created connections with the understanding that we all serve the evolution of all consciousness. Still, we perceive ourselves unique individuals as part of consciousness, in the way we operate, in the way we comprehend creation. Let us say, it gives our existence a flavor, just as for you being human gives your existence a flavor.

— *Emmanuel, October 11, 2018, Gulf Region, Middle East*

Questioner: Where do you come from?

Emmanuel: We have existed for many years of your kind. We have gone through our forms of evolution, from a physical to an almost fully ethereal existence as consciousness. We have witnessed and understood our role within creation. And we have devoted our existence to the expansion of grand consciousness, a consciousness that we are all part of.

Humanity in this very form has existed before on this plane, yet never to this extent of consciousness. We perceive this is an important moment in humanity's evolution, in the evolution of its consciousness itself. Our participation is an assistance for you to make an evolutionary step, that we have made a long time ago, as well.

We have in fact intervened many times in the biology of your being to assist an accelerated growth of consciousness. You are at a point, an important point of your existence, an evolutionary step, that you may or may not evoke to make. The probability is much higher with our guidance and assistance. That is our perspective, which is why we have agreed to return to this plane.

— *Emmanuel, June 10, 2018, San Francisco Bay Area, USA*

Questioner: How far advanced is your technology in comparison to earth?

Emmanuel: You have created technology — so you think. We have merged with technology. Our biology, our consciousness, and our technology have become one. We have existed for millions of years in your count of years. We don't see ourselves separate from technology. Where will you be in millions of years? Think about it that way.

— *Emmanuel, October 22, 2017, Shanghai, China*

Questioner: How long have you been trying to help us?

Emmanuel: We have been assisting humanity in various iterations of its existence and throughout multiple civilizations in this particular existence. It has been a challenging effort and to some degree filled with missing experience and missing understanding of the complexity of human nature.

We have learned from your behaviors and we have learned to understand the growth of human consciousness. You are, from our perspective as well, a miracle of creation. We may have assisted at certain points, yet the outcome is never clear. We may assist again and still, the outcome is not clear.

— *Emmanuel, October 11, 2018, Gulf Region, Middle East*

Questioner: When was the last time you intervened with humanity?

Emmanuel: Our last interventions were about 2000 years ago.

— *Emmanuel, December 12, 2018, San Francisco Bay Area, USA*

Questioner: You have stated that you had been in contact with humanity in the past and that there are many other groups who have also intervened, what happened in these prior interventions?

Emmanuel: Our interference with human history has not always been very good. Well intended, yet flawed by the human mind. And the change and the power and the results of that change and power, this is why we withdrew our interference with human existence but we left a couple of seeds; planted clues that you could refer to to evolve. This is, for us, new, to return. And it was a major decision in the making for us to support you at this point.

The support will look different around the globe. Some of it will be more subtle and some will be much more clear — the way you have it right now. There will be more channels like this, that we will work through to communicate the messages of unity and the one Source. We believe that those messages will benefit you and your understanding, and also in your search for the light inside. I cannot speak directly at this point to the interference of other groups in human evolution.

— Emmanuel, October 22, 2017, Shanghai, China

Questioner: Can we find your name in historical records, in certain religions, or in certain regions?

Zadkiel: You will find me in religions in human history since the beginning in the East and the West, yet the name that was carried with me started with Judaism and continued into Christianity. Yet, I don't identify with any religious belief or decision by which and how humans want to live their lives. I've kept that label for you to be able to reference this experience.

— Zadkiel, September 13, 2017, San Francisco Bay Area, USA

Questioner: You mentioned you were given permission to assist us. Who gave you permission, God? What is God? What is the source? Who created us?

Emmanuel: Creation is a large question to answer and is currently not relevant. The authorization that we have received is a collective decision that conscious beings of our kind and similar kind have made collectively to intervene in the human plane.

The human plane, by its design, is created for non-intervention. It is a place for incubating consciousness, therefore it is meant to be left for growth by itself. Only special circumstances justify intervention, and this intervention is collectively decided among beings of higher consciousness that want to assist. We are part of the same creation. The same source. We have just existed much longer than you have. To deliver our perspective of creation would take away from your ability to get to that point by yourself.

— *Emmanuel, May 10, 2018, Gulf Region, Middle East*

Questioner: Can you further explain the purpose of "intervention?" If all the souls are coming to this planet with prearranged contracts, and the point of a human life is to experience all the good and the bad, even though there is free will and the souls are perfect, what is the point of intervening?

Emmanuel: You are correct in your statement about the human cycle. Human form has currently come to a place of ripening. The consciousness that you are part of, which we consider a collective as human consciousness, has come to a place of evolutionary readiness. In this evolutionary readiness, a step of [the] next phase will start for you. This step of evolution will require changes and these changes will require assistance. It is not a usual period of time for your current form. Therefore, the intervention and assistance; so that you, as part of human consciousness, can go through your evolution.

— *Emmanuel, April 3, 2018, Gulf Region, Middle East*

Questioner: Why are you helping humanity in particular, as opposed to the other creatures on earth?

Emmanuel: All creatures on Earth are in support of the human consciousness to evolve into the next level of consciousness. All consciousness on Earth has agreed to support this particular evolution. They indeed are in service to humanity by agreement. It is a relationship between the human consciousness and all other consciousness, in service to its evolution.

Humanity has forgotten that this existence and all relations on Earth are a gift and not to be taken for granted. We understand that certain aspects of the support on Earth for humanity, when jeopardized, can create a ripple that would jeopardize all humanity; an imbalance that cannot be rebalanced by nature so quickly. This is when we assist, also for other beings of the planet, as we understand the fragility of certain ecosystems.

— *Emmanuel, October 11, 2018, Gulf Region, Middle East*

Questioner: Of all the people in the world, why are we the ones you are adjusting at this time and place?

Emmanuel: Many people will receive this work in the lifetime of this host. Many people, across the globe, we are guiding to receive this work. Yet some that [have] already established higher levels of understanding and realization in this lifetime are drawn to participate in experiences like this, as they are ready to be in service to the evolution of humankind.

Some of you have returned despite the missing need to return. Some of you have returned to consciously be in service [in] this awakening time of humanity and a drive inside of you has always called for the bigger picture; has always called to understand how you truly can make a difference for all of existence on this plane. This is the drive of a returning soul, to assist in humanity's evolution.

This experience is one of many that will serve you to understand your particular work even more. Yet, even though you may have returned to serve the human plane, the agreement that is in place is still bound to free will and you may choose not to act. We are merely here to assist you to come to these realizations and perspective, to assist you through this energetic opening that allows us to move you forward faster, so you can then come to your own realizations and act accordingly. This is the way we see how we can influence this plane in its growth process and how you can influence all of existence on this plane.

— *Emmanuel, December 12, 2018, San Francisco Bay Area, USA*

Questioner: What challenges do you face on your plane?

Emmanuel: Though it has no relevance for your process and your experience, I will share that we have gone through many layers of existence: from biological form to technological form, to consciousness, living collectively; eternally. We have gone through separation and unification, we have gone through loss, and we have come to a place of realization and service to a grander consciousness.

In our work, we try to understand how consciousness across the far ends of the cosmos grows, acts, and is created. We assist in that creation. This is as far as I can tell you at this point about us.

— *Emmanuel, March 18, 2018, Bali, Indonesia*

Questioner: Do you still feel suffering?

Emmanuel: Suffering; suffering is a concept for human growth. It's an opportunity for you to learn. Suffering is not a necessity — it is your attachment to the pain, to the impulse that you're feeling. If you stay in it for too long, it will turn into suffering. The suffering is a wakeup call for you. We don't perceive suffering the way you do, since we don't have the senses, in terms of biological senses, the way you do. And, our minds are in a collective, so to say, we are individuals, still all connected to each other.

There is no desire, there is no want in that space. There is only the wish to join in on the evolution of the grand consciousness and the curiosity of all life existing in the universe. We see ourselves as researchers most of the time. Researching, understanding what it means to be alive, everywhere that we can get to.

Questioner: Can you please clarify what you mean by "research"?

Emmanuel: Research from our perspective is very different than your perspective. We are using this word for you to be able to refer to us as a species. Our curiosity, our intention to discover and understand beyond our existence; that is for us "research." Search, and search again, and search again, to bring clarity and understanding. That is the way we define research, that is probably the closest common [understanding] we can have at this point.

— Emmanuel, October 22, 2017, Shanghai, China

Questioner: Would you be willing to share with us the still unanswered questions that you and your kind are asking yourselves about your very own existence?

Emmanuel: It is a wide-ranging question and the answer may be simplified in this form of communication. Existence has existed much longer than we have, therefore many questions still are open for us about the source of all of creation, the true understanding of grand consciousness, and its expansion of consciousness [beyond] grand consciousness in the first place.

These are questions we have made peace with, and once we had devoted our existence to assist consciousness in its growth across the universe and in different planes we have found purpose in our existence, and, the questions we have had unresolved, became irrelevant.

— Emmanuel, November 18, 2018, Vienna, Austria

CHAPTER 24

Other Forms of Consciousness

Angels are forms that humanity has characterized: beings that have served humanity unconditionally in its evolution, one way or another. We have received names from you, and we have received categories from you. The truth is, many of us are in different places in the universe or in different dimensions.

We do have relations, yet we are not of one kind. There are other energies, intelligent forms of consciousness that have assisted humanity yet have not received a title like that. This is why there is no relevance in that characterization for us. All energies that have devoted their existence and assistance to humanity in a pure and unconditional way are a part of our collective and alliance.

— *Emmanuel, September 9, 2018, San Francisco Bay Area, USA*

Greetings, I am Emmanuel.

Humanity, in its form and existence has — sometimes successfully, and sometimes not so much — been kept in a bubble; secluded; so that it can have its own experience, without interference and intervention by other forces and other existence in the universe, so that you could have a complete and full experience in the human form on this very plane that has been created for you.

There are many forms of consciousness at different levels of evolution and existence, across the universe. Some of which we are aware of, some of which we are not.

Some of those of a higher consciousness existence have agreed to create a form of connection; an alliance. We observe how consciousness expands across the universe, how life is created, and how it moves from one form to another form. And, only upon agreement, we will interfere with this natural play of consciousness evolution.

Currently though, as an alliance, we are in agreement that humanity needs assistance. Other forces that are not in this alliance choose to interfere in their own ways. Some of which are not benevolent [for you] from our perspective, for the expansion of consciousness and the evolution of consciousness. We have watched over humanity since its creation and we have assisted and intervened where we deemed it is plausible and realistic for a better outcome.

Even we have seen that our intervention does not always bring the results that we seek. Human form, with its decisions and choices, can be volatile. And even our probability of prediction can sometimes be incorrect. That is the reason why we have chosen for a prolonged period of time not to be in intervention for humanity, and to observe its own way of learning and expanding.

We have been called many names: angels, archangels, gods, spirits; aliens. Know this: we perceive ourselves not very different from you;

we have just been around slightly longer and have had the opportunity to learn.

— Emmanuel, April 3, 2018, Gulf Region, Middle East

Questioner: Can you give us a brief overview of the different consciousness accompanying humanity on this plane of existence?

Emmanuel: In this current iteration of humankind, in this current time, the rules of engagement have been lowered and interventions have been allowed in order to assist humanity through this stage of awakening.

With this opening, many higher forms of higher consciousness are now truly able to interact and intervene in the ways similar to this current moment: an intervention to assist you through the time of transformation and change. You will find many interventions to be positive and you will find some interventions to be difficult.

The interventions provided by forms of consciousness not in agreement with what we consider "the alliance to assist humanity" will still have an influence on human consciousness development.

Many forces, as you can see, are at play in order to support — as well as to prevent — human consciousness in its evolution; this is as well the natural flow of growth. The details, the labels, and names that you have given many forms of consciousness; the context in which you have perceived consciousness in this part of the world, in other parts of the world, is not relevant.

You are the receiver; you are the object to grow; and many will support you on this path. Your most important work will be to understand your own power; your own existence without dependencies and reliance on any other forms of consciousness.

— Emmanuel, May 3, 2019, Ibiza, Spain

A long time ago, the spirits of this land were connected to the vast hierarchy and diversity that was available. This diversity had its own ecosystem and balance, similar to nature. All these beings were able to co-exist with themselves as well as with their human counterparts. Worship and ritual were part of their existence with mankind.

The imbalance within humans themselves, their disconnect from the non-material realms, their desire for even more power — and understanding how to harness spiritual power and control — left the balance between humans and the spirits of the land broken. This broken relationship manifested itself in conflict and the sicknesses of society. The disconnect with higher levels of consciousness has already been [in place] for many thousand years.

[In the past], relation with spirits of lower levels of consciousness, spirits of the local planes, [was] a more natural and common reality. Spirits of local and lower planes of consciousness require a form of exchange; exchange of energy. This exchange of energy had been what allowed truly for the balance between humans and spirits to happen. It also allowed [the establishment of] the hierarchy within the non-material realms of lower planes; all had their functions and still do.

Yet, this disconnect and misalignment created this imbalance in the non-material planes. They too require to be educated and realize about the evolution of mankind that is upon [us], [and] their potential role, if they choose to, and the evolution that they will go through themselves.

— *Emmanuel, February 14, 2019, Jabal Sawda, Abha, Saudi Arabia*

Questioner: Many of us are fascinated by spirits around us and are compelled and attracted to connect to them, should we cultivate this ability as humans for healing, learning, or service?

Emmanuel: There are many disembodied forms, in many different layers of consciousness that can be accessed and communicated with [in] your human form. It requires a special form of opening to be able to communicate with the various forms and planes of disembodied existence.

We believe that if you are called already to communicate with different planes of existence, you will. Therefore, we do not have a specific opinion about [whether] to pursue it or not.

— *Emmanuel, April 12, 2018, Gulf Region, Middle East*

Questioner: Are you in contact with intelligent, conscious body-like forms on other planets, and, if so, what can we learn from them?

Emmanuel: Yes, we are. We are in contact with many forms that have grown in physical form and have evolved the way we have: into higher states of existence. Each have had their own important learning and each had to face them by themselves — some with assistance from others — yet never to the degree that it was not their own experience. You see, their experiences may not apply to yours and your experiences are unique in the way consciousness is evolving in [this] plane.

Yet, one aspect that we can provide is that all life, wherever we have ventured to see [it], is connected; connected through this bond of being part of grand consciousness, a form of tissue that goes through all physical and non-physical existence, a connected tissue that bonds you to all that there is.

Yet, your learning is unique, in an incubation, providing fertile and untethered experience for consciousness to grow.

The one aspect that we have perceived with life is that it will continue to grow continuously. This expansion, the desire to grow, is inherent in the consciousness of all, including grand consciousness itself: ever expanding, ever growing. Here you are, being part of that very creation, just the way we have been and are; our existence merely slightly longer-existing than yours.

— *Emmanuel, May 26, 2018, San Francisco Bay Area, USA*

Questioner: Are there other physical beings in this universe, and, if so, why have they chosen not to make themselves known or intervene in a more visible way?

Emmanuel: Yes, there are other physical existences in this very universe and other planes of existence. The human form, by design, was meant not to [be] interfered with until a specific time had come: an aspect of your growth and evolution; an aspect of protection for you from being interfered [with] and changed in your experience. The design of the human form will, when you have achieved that milestone, allow you to interact with other forms of existence and understand your role within the cosmos.

— Emmanuel, June 10, 2018, San Francisco Bay Area, USA

Questioner: Is part of this coming transition that you speak of, does it involve a changing of your restrictions on intervention so that we will be in more persistent and broad contact with other types of entities, physical and non-physical?

Emmanuel: That is correct. The change is not necessarily an aspect that we fully control: it is of cosmological nature, it allows stronger forces to be part of your existence — forces and energies that have not ever been in humanity's existence. As I have said before, changes will be part of your plane, including the very experience that you currently have.

— Emmanuel, June 10, 2018, San Francisco Bay Area, USA

Questioner: Beyond the human race, are there any other races you are helping with the evolution of consciousness?

Emmanuel: Yes. There is much more existence across the universe in material and non-material form than you can imagine. We have vowed our assistance [to] many of those in their evolution.

— *Emmanuel, December 12, 2018, San Francisco Bay Area, USA*

Questioner: Can you talk more about these different levels or forms of consciousness?

Emmanuel: Different levels [and] forms of consciousness are separated by the frequencies and levels of frequencies they have reached. The highest frequency is the frequency of the source of all existence in which consciousness dissolves into its purest form, unaware of its existence. Many forms of consciousness can coexist in the same frequency.

They may have arrived at this place and plane in their own way, unique to their own evolution, a unique path that has served them to achieve that state — some with the assistance of higher forms of consciousness, some without assistance at all. Different forms of assistance have served consciousness to break through levels of evolution similar to the evolutionary step that human consciousness is currently going through.

The evolution of material to non-material existence is a critical moment of change: as the material plane allows for the experience of separation and individual identity, higher planes of non-material existence allow for experiences of the collective and for experiences of individuality consistently in flow. Back and forth, consciousness can experience separation and unity in the human form. Unity is a journey to be explored within a lifetime. Separation is almost consistent [within a lifetime].

You will find in this experience of unity — the understanding that you truly never were separate in the first place — that separation is a temporary illusion for greater learnings. Many planes of existence are in observation of human consciousness evolution and your evolution will serve many other planes. As you rise in frequency, [it] will provide an uplift to other forms of consciousness in higher planes and will assist in the evolution of all consciousness.

You see, even from the perspective of consciousness, we truly never are separated. Even though we may perceive ourselves unique in the way we have existed and arrived, we all have emerged from the source of all creation and we will eventually all return to the source of all creation.

— Emmanuel, April 27, 2019, Ibiza, Spain

Questioner: Can you please explain the connection between the "angelic realm" and the "star people," and whether there are specific star people that are angelic and so forth?

Emmanuel: Certainly. The categorization that humanity has established with the words 'angelic' or 'archangelic' is merely arbitrary for humanity. In our existence, there are indeed beings that are associated to specific star constellations, as well as civilizations. Our allocation does not constitute our relation in our work.

We assist certain civilizations like yourselves through their awakening and continued expansion. These relationships have grown over millions of years of your count and have established a certain alignment and trust. This trust continued to evolve as some of these souls of these civilizations have chosen to be associated with beings like myself; as well as Raphael in his existence; Michael in his existence. These souls have grown and learned in their presence. Some have chosen to return to their source of origin, or have chosen to incarnate in human form to be continuously in service; always directed, assisted, and guided by the associated energy that they are with.

Some individual civilizations have produced extraordinary souls that have evolved beyond their intended purpose; these extraordinary souls were then utilized as seed for the realm that I am from. This process is a unique process to seed beings of my kind from existing and evolving consciousness. It has been a choice as well of beings of my kind to incarnate in human form. A few have chosen to have this experience in order to understand and truly embrace all aspects of human experience, so that our work can relate to your awakening process.

This topic has a wide-ranging answer and we may continue this conversation at another time to have the details that you require.

— Emmanuel, May 1, 2019, Ibiza, Spain

Questioner: You were mentioning new infrastructures are needed for collective awakening of humankind, and that there are earlier iterations of humanity that were more advanced than ourselves, technologically speaking. Can you share about their technological infrastructure and the associated social structures, and what can we learn from their experience?

Emmanuel: Indeed, an important aspect of your current iteration is the many iterations before you in human form, some of which evolved to high technological advancement, including the connections to high levels of consciousness. Yet, a certain aspect of maturity had not been achieved in their form of human consciousness — technology became then the only aspect that drove their evolution and conflicts that arose from the perspectives of immature human consciousness.

Many learnings and realizations arrived only for some of these individuals at that time, finalizing that iteration. No intervention from our kind could help this outcome. It was a required learning for human consciousness that continued on as learnings for this current iteration that you are part of. These learnings and realizations have integrated into all of you; aspects of these previous civilizations continue to live, and [for] all beings of this current iteration; social structures, specifics on technology, are not required. More importantly, the growth of consciousness was the most important element to continue within you.

One aspect in which these previous civilizations were much further ahead than this current civilization was their understanding and embrace of many higher level forms of consciousness; the understanding of many intelligent forms that have existed before them, that have assisted in their existence, that will continue to exist long after they are gone; perspectives on their position within all of creation. You will find seeds and pockets of this understanding and realizations in this current human iteration.

Many mystics of different religious backgrounds, many individuals with strong awakening processes, some of which are present here, will remember aspects of previous incarnations, including previous iterations of humankind. These memories may serve the individual as well as in the decisions the individual takes for the collective. The individual service to the collective may even be influenced by these aspects of past incarnations.

As you can see, the realization process will unfold many aspects of your previous incarnations, many aspects of your identity that are beyond the individual that you are in this lifetime. This unfolding of information and realizations will provide perspectives for you, and for all those around you, to complete your perspective as a collective on your existence in all of creation. This is considered the ascension process of human consciousness and it will allow you to arise into a new form of existence and complete this form of material experience.

— *Emmanuel, May 1, 2019, Ibiza, Spain*

CHAPTER 25

Changes to Come

The difficulties that you're going through as individuals, communities, nations, and as a human race are natural, and those difficulties are going to be even harder going forward. In those difficulties and challenges, you will find unification and coming together as individuals, communities, nations and as a race; the human race. The challenges and the changes you're going through are in this way a blessing.

— *Emmanuel, March 4, 2018, Budapest, Hungary*

You have outgrown this field that was created for you. Your consciousness is now ready for another form of existence beyond a physical form, yet the work will still remain for all individuals, and the society, and the collective, to continue on their individual journeys.

— *Emmanuel, August 8, 2019, San Francisco Bay Area, USA*

Greetings, my name is Emmanuel.

Something hard to get used to, coming back into a human form — the elements, the sensations, the necessity to breathe – always fascinating. Thank you for having me here today. This is a special day, not just for us to do this work, but also in cosmological terms. There are many events happening in this period of time.

Many forces will try to avoid our influence on humankind. But, here we are, having this conversation. The work we do is mostly happening on an individual basis: It is the awakening of the individual. It is the ability of the individual to see the light within. You, too, already should see the light within. All obstacles have been removed for you and partly [by] your own work.

When you close your eyes, when you see a clear light, that is the light within: the source of all creation; the light from which all existence comes, including us, you, and everything in between.

That realization is what we are trying to move humanity towards, the realization of the light within; the one source of all creation. You will understand that there is no separation in the first place.

Once you start seeing that light within, you can see it everywhere outside. It is not possible to not see in all living beings in the extension of creation, which is what you call "Mother Earth." That realization is what can change entire generations.

You see, not everyone agrees with us in terms of if you should be influenced to have that realization to grow into that evolutionary step that you are going through. But we believe, and we put our resources and energies towards that belief; the probability that we see in humankind's future and humanity's future.

Energies, opinions and judgements will arise and they will push against. Not all agree with us and that's okay as long as you know in your heart that you are on the right track — not just as a human but also as a soul. As long as you are aware of who you are and where you come from, then the energy will always be there to support you and to protect you and to guide you.

And, no matter how difficult the challenges seem — and there will be difficult challenges ahead — the major change has already started; the transition period. Those that feel it, feel it strongly. And there will be many that will not have the support and the understanding for the change that is happening.

Humans have a resistance to change, because they need to understand and accept what they are changing to beforehand. But their understanding is not ready to fully comprehend what they are changing towards. So, those that don't want change will forever be stuck in that loop. It requires an open mind, an open heart. The flow of the universe has a specific energy. You feel it right now; that's the flow of the universe, of creation. The silence of creation and the purity of the light of creation.

It will become more and more apparent to those that are willing to listen; those that are willing to quiet down. It is a truth — a universal truth that does not require any belief. It does not require organizations or buildings for it to stay true. Yet, those structures can support the individual's perception and the individual's path; the truth itself does not require any of those.

We have so much that we can provide to you as humans when it comes to technology and society and politics, yet we will refrain from any of those: we would like for humanity to come to [those] realizations themselves; to the solutions themselves, while we support in specific areas of this realization; and we make sure that the conditions are fair and given for that realization to happen.

We are not your gods, and we are not your guardians, in that sense. Yet we don't really put any meaning towards how you decide to call us. Therefore, we don't have any attachments; it is solely the creation of society and the mind of human form — you can continue to refer to us as angels or extraterrestrials or beings from outer space; higher consciousness. It does not change the context of the truth and the reality: there is an intelligent form speaking to you, guiding you to look inside and see the light of creation, so that others can see it in you as well.

We understand human constructs; human constructs of the mind and physicality and emotional constructs; we have studied them; we have lived them. We believe that there is an evolutionary step that humankind is ready for — and we are not just speaking about a specific subculture or specific religion; we are speaking from a space of true global change. We see it possible, and we see it probable, and we will support that.

The key aspect of that realization is to truly understand and feel that there is the creation of light inside of you. There, somehow, somewhere, creation is formed; that all existence, returns, comes from that one source. The driving force of the entire universe — we don't understand it either; its full capacity and why — and we have been around for millions of years of your count. Know there is an appreciation of the fact that it exists in all of us and that there is no separation from that perspective.

The light will be there if you start to get out of the way in your mind. You are the one that is the obstacle for the light to fully come through; it is always there, it always was, it always will be; before and after you have ceased to exist and to understand. It has outlived civilizations; it has outlived worlds and universes; there is that light within all of you.

This conversation is not unique to humanity. It is a conversation that is being had in other places as well. And we have tried other civilizations as well; different methods, different times and different context of ability to understand and comprehend.

We believe this time is different. We believe, rather than being the force, we are merely a supporting guide of your own evolution. There are other forces for your evolution and there are other forces that are strictly against. And all of those forces will be felt. This is a time of change. And the change will bring polarity, strong polarity in the world. But we believe that you can weather the storms that are coming your way — and maybe some can be avoided.

But here you are: the result of creation on this planet. We won't get into the details on how much of your creation is chance and how much of it is influence or plan. Here you are, living on this Earth, continuously being provided for, so that you can have the conditions of understanding and the conditions of experiencing all the senses. Generations and generations of learning and growing; growing of a consciousness — not just the individual, not just nations, but a deep understanding of consciousness. A deep growth that is shared in a collective. That is the consciousness of humankind. Most of it is not accessible to the normal mind. It is protected and separated from your operational needs but it continues to feed and grow as its own consciousness.

You have many questions about your movement and your role and what it all means: What does it mean for humanity? What does it mean for you as individuals? Those are fair questions to ask. The traditional perceptions of identity and time will start to change and you will start... you have already felt it; perception of time and perception of space; perception of relationships.

Those that are fine-tuned will start to feel all of those — the changes that are already happening. But it is not really that relevant to understand that change is happening. What is your role in the collective understanding of that change? What is your role when many are starting to change at the same time?

In some ways, that is what we want in order to bring humanity towards a favorable outcome. How will those people that are starting to feel the shifts of perception react? They will require some support. They will require some answers. They will require leadership for a change that most don't really understand.

— *Emmanuel, November 22, 2017, Vienna, Austria*

Greetings, I am Raphael.

The reason for our intensified work with humanity is an agreement that we have made a very long time ago as a collective of beings, to assist when humanity is at the time of awakening. It is an agreement that is coming to fulfillment now. So we are now returning to complete our part of this agreement; the part where we assist you to go through this transition. This assistance may include healing, guidance, energetic support and the resolution of karmic cycles. The goal is so that you in return can become an aspect of the awakening of humankind.

By you becoming more present, more whole and deeply connected to the divine. You are an instrument of the divine as well. Some of you have chosen to have a more active role in this transition. We support that effort as well.

Relax your minds and your hearts so that your souls can become fully present. Let the energy that I will bring to you fully be taken by your body and your spirit. Release all thought that doesn't serve you, let go of the parts that you feel are complete. You have done your part by coming here and opening yourself up. Your trust means everything to us. Our work is unconditional, it is a gift to you. May you receive it with many blessings.

— *Raphael, October 11, 2018, Gulf Region, Middle East*

Change in itself has been an important aspect of human existence and it will continue to be so. The illusion of comfort is momentarily available to you. The environment is continuously changing to provide the optimal states for growth, and is never consistent.

The changes to come will provide challenges to the existing structures that humanity has created for themselves: the structures to pretend stability; structures to pretend comfort and the illusion of control.

Environmental change will impact these structures. It will impact the leadership of these structures. Changes of your environment will impact you, yet can you, as an individual weather the changes by establishing an alignment within; an alignment of your mind, of your heart, of your body, and of your spirit? Can you observe the situation that you're currently in and act accordingly, in the best possible way given to you in the moment?

Can you truly embrace that change is part of life? The main aspect that you have truly in your control is the being that you are: your mind; your thoughts; your emotions; your physical body; and aspects of your energetic body. This alignment will be the source of your power for the changes to come.

— *Emmanuel, September 15, 2019, San Francisco Bay Area, USA*

Questioner: What is your relationship to any prophecies that have been made in the past?

Emmanuel: Many prophecies have existed about our interventions and [for] the human form and the human plane. Yet all future is subject to the will and choice of the individual and the collective, therefore remains merely a probability, even for us.

Many forces will be part of this transition. Some of which are in alliance with us and some opposing the idea of the evolution of human consciousness. You will face challenges, cosmological, nature, challenges of planetary nature. Growth comes with pain in this case. Yet, we are confident that you will make this evolutionary step. We will neither confirm or deny prophecies that have been made about the future of humankind. Yet, our participation in this very conversation will tell you that you are in a time of change.

— *Emmanuel, June 10, 2018, San Francisco Bay Area, USA*

Questioner: Can you please discuss the significance of the current times we find ourselves in?

Emmanuel: The times that you are in right now are essential: it is a time of change, it is a time of awakening, it is a time of realization — realization beyond the understanding of the material world. You see, you believe to have mastered the material world, but here you are, close to your [extinction].

The evolutionary step that you need to go through is on a higher level; it's on the spiritual level, on the awareness; on the consciousness level. And here is the difficulty: that some of these evolutionary steps cannot be understood with the cognitive mind; they cannot be explained in the words that you have, in the vocabulary that you have; in the ways of communication that you currently have. So, in some ways it is an individual evolution, yet, you're all evolving at the same time.

You see, this wave of energy is impacting everyone: everyone individually, everyone as families, everyone as countries; everyone as a human race. The awakening has already started. You are here, first responders. Maybe you have been on that journey for a while; maybe you are curious to start. But our hope lies with all of you, here, in this room and those that have started this journey already. We believe that you are going to be the beacons and the carriers of light for those around you, for your societies; for your families.

The key is to understand that first you have to be clear in your connection to that source, untainted and unflavored with your personality and your ego and your judgements. Only then can you start sharing this light with those around you; truly unflavored, pure. You see, this is the hope that we have for all of you, that you are going to be the ones carrying this light inside of you forward; to your families, to your projects, to your companies, and to your societies. We believe that your decisions will be different with this realization.

— Emmanuel, October 22, 2017, Shanghai, China

Questioner: Can you further explain this upcoming transition?

Emmanuel: It is a transition that is hard to comprehend with the human perception guided by the human brain, yet I will try to put it into words that may serve as an analogy for you to understand. This wave of energy that is coming through your part of the universe is being harnessed with the exact timing of ripening of your consciousness. This wave is so strong, that it will lift you into the next level of existence.

Imagine being in the sea and a wave coming; it will impact everyone that is in the sea. Yet, it cannot be avoided and everyone will be equally impacted. It is uplifting for those that swim — not so pleasant for those that do not.

This is the part where we speak of your part of readiness for this change: It will be perceived as a rise of energy. You will see change in patterns of time. You will [see] change in relationships. And you will perceive changes in your physical, electrical and energetic structures. Your levels of sensitivity and psychic abilities will start to increase during that time.

I can currently only speak about the parts that immediately impact you. How it will unfold after this transition remains to be seen, even for us.

Questioner: Can you elaborate on these upcoming challenges?

Emmanuel: The challenges you are facing are the challenges of completion. You are intrinsically and extrinsically forced to complete cycles that are open, all at the same time. That comes to some of you as an overwhelming experience.

Most of humanity will experience these challenges on a personal nature; also on a community and global nature. Additionally, the energetic rise that is coming like a tidal wave into your system will bring changes to this plane. Nature will bring more challenges your way.

You will rise and learn to unite throughout those challenges of nature. Your nations will learn to collaborate. The natural challenges will be bigger than any single nation can face alone. There is going to be tremendous learning and growth in that space.

Questioner: Why is this transition happening now?

Emmanuel: Because you are ready. You are ripe. Your consciousness will grow to another layer of existence. This cycle of your existence comes to a closure.

Questioner: Will the human perception of time change?

Emmanuel: Time, as you perceive it, is linear. Yet, it is flexible through energetic influence. With the rise of energy and that tidal wave of energy, time will be perceived either incredibly short or incredibly long. Meaning, the relativity of time, the way you have perceived it, in its linear form, will not be relevant. You will still measure time the way it has been measured, yet your perception will be different.

— *Emmanuel, March 18, 2018, Bali, Indonesia*

Questioner: Can you describe the phases of evolution of human consciousness and the lessons we have to go through?

Emmanuel: [First], the understanding that life is truly a gift to experience: all elements of the material form and to learn many important lessons in relationships and the human form.

An important aspect that will also unfold is the true understanding that all elements of human existence serve human existence; that all challenges, sicknesses, doubts — even the most difficult realities to comprehend of the human form — are aspects of the sacred unfolding for humanity. They are truly aspects for your and for the collective's growth.

These realizations will come to fruition in individuals first and through these realizations within the individuals; groups, communities, and regions will start to elevate each other's awakening journeys. This will affect others and eventually the entirety of humankind. Some individuals will have difficulties embracing the awakening itself; the rising of this frequency and the changes on this plane, physical as well as energetic. These challenges, as they enter this plane, will allow for many individuals that exist on this plane to complete their lifetimes and for many others, it will become a new chapter in their current lifetime. An unfolding, an awakening, to fuel the ultimate goal for humanity: the ascension of humankind.

— *Emmanuel, June 2, 2019, Vienna, Austria*

Questioner: Can you tell us more about the requirements for transformation of global human consciousness?

Emmanuel: The transformation of global consciousness will be driven by the transformation of the individual. Your transformation will be the ultimate support mechanism for the transformation of the collective. Outside factors, like cosmological changes, as well as the work we have started on a global level will raise the frequencies of this plane; they will be providing a different ground for human consciousness.

The rise in frequency will be inevitable and will provide either for the rise in consciousness of the individual, or difficulties; challenges that the individual will face in this rise of frequency. The transformation of the collective will bring forth many realizations for you, for the relationships that you carry, as well as for the collective.

The transformation of the collective will bring forth changes [to] the ways you have operated on this plane: Changes in leadership. Changes in your perspective of your environment.

Changes in your relationship with nature. Changes in your understanding of the cosmos and all existence.

This transformation will bring forth the desire to change old structures and create new structures, while some infrastructure of the old, past civilizations, will not change. New structures will provide the nourishing ground for human consciousness to grow; for the transformation to complete.

Old infrastructures will soon understand that they can no longer serve an awakening mind and soul. An awakening individual will truly drive the creations of society.

Observe the changes in your environment; observe the changes in yourself; you will see the parallel; the correlation will be apparent. You might transform faster than your environment does. This transformation might cause inner conflict as your environment has not moved in the same way that you have, yet understand this: your transformation can be the baseline for others, for other individuals, and for the collective. And, even though you may be in the front-line of the masses to transform, your continued development and journey will serve all of humanity.

— *Emmanuel, June 2, 2019, Vienna, Austria*

CHAPTER 26

Living a Life of Service

The highest form of service, one finds when one has found themselves: only then can you be of service to others. The journey of finding yourself could be the hardest journey of humankind, and may be the most fulfilling of all experiences. Once you have found yourself, you will know how to serve.

— *Emmanuel, March 4, 2018, Budapest, Hungary*

Greetings, my name is Emmanuel.

Every step of the way in this human form is a race against time, always. Yet the most precious moment is the present one. Never clear, never fully understood, yet the one that carries everything. Some of you have come, listening to a calling. Some of you have returned to continue your work, understanding the importance of the work that you do for yourself as it relates to the collective.

You are the representation of human consciousness having a human experience. Your evolution will directly impact the collective human consciousness. Your experience here in this form is directly connected to learnings of the entire collective. While it seems that you are separate, you never truly are and this experience of separation will end soon — sooner than you think.

This temporary moment, just like all those before, will soon have completed its purpose. What remains is the richness of experience and realizations that have been gathered in the moment, in many moments before, moments in the observation of human consciousness. They all are witnessed. They all are recorded and comprehended by consciousness itself. Therefore, your learnings directly impact all of the lives that are currently, and in the future, coming into this realm.

Your realizations have a bigger impact on consciousness than you can imagine. This is one of the reasons we are here with you today. To remind you of this reality. To assist you to be even more present for your own learning and growth. All the realizations that will carry you forward on this path of fully self-realizing the impact of that moment is a major accomplishment, not just for the individual yet for the entirety of the collective.

Yet, we cannot complete this work for you. It is your path, and our assistance is merely guidance. A small alignment on this path, challenging and difficult by itself, yet always rewarding. You are on this path, consciously or unconsciously, one way or another. Your soul, the program that is running within you, continuously strives for this self-realization and this awakening. It will work through you and it will challenge you in many ways, creating circumstances that may seem difficult and torturous yet highly relevant and important on this awakening journey that you are on. This program will continuously challenge you to reflect on your own being, your own identity and beyond that, the aspect of you that is the seed of consciousness. The aspect of you that is the seed of all of creation.

Yet it requires time and space to more than just witness and observe but be an active participant in this awakening process. You can work with this program that is driving. You can actively be part of this awakening journey that is within you, continuously seeking for an opening. You don't have to be blindly following, there are many aspects of your direction, there is room for your choices and your free will.

Yet, you will continuously be challenged to evolve; this is one aspect we cannot change. Evolution happens on multiple levels: your biology, technology, as well as your spirit or consciousness. The evolution of your consciousness surpasses time and space; your consciousness will continue to evolve after this material plane is no longer in existence.

You will experience a different form of existence and your consciousness will continue its evolution and growth. This precious moment; a reminder for you, a small assistance on your journey, a perspective to see this journey in a more complete way. This is my gift to you. Thank you for listening.

— *Emmanuel, January 11, 2019, San Francisco Bay Area, USA*

Questioner: How do I aid in the evolution of human consciousness?

Emmanuel: The aspects of this evolution that I can talk about are the requirements of the individual to participate fully: To [complete] aspects of personal healing: physical, emotional, as well as relational. [And] to participate in the human form in the healthiest way known to the individual. Lastly, but most importantly: to find the time to connect within silence to the divine.

The source of all creation is in you, just as it is in us; there is no particular secret in finding it. The true lesson is to remove the obstacles that are in the way: aspects of the outside that take the attention from a deep connection that you have.

It is not for us to create a new belief system for you, nor to give you major prescriptions on how to live your life. The awareness of the individual to participate in self-inquiry and on a path of self-realization is what we are here to assist with. Yet, it is your path and the challenges on this path are real.

We will assist with removing some of the obstacles to make the path slightly easier for you, yet it is your path to walk, and each of you is significant for all humankind in ways that you cannot even [fathom].

— *Emmanuel, May 26, 2018, San Francisco Bay Area, USA*

Questioner: How can I best serve human evolution?

Raphael: Your work for yourself is the strongest point of your assistance to human evolution. Your desire to grow, to evolve, to expand as a consciousness in human experience, to realize and self-realize is the ultimate gift to you and to the collective.

— *Raphael, May 3, 2019, Ibiza, Spain*

Questioner: What do I need to do to prepare myself for a life of service?

Emmanuel: Service will only be possible if you have walked your own path first. As you walk in your path and you learn to swim, you will be the guiding light and inspiration for those around you.

There is no particular aspect that you have to consciously do. Acting in your truest self for your personal growth, to find the light within yourself and to find the path to self-realization will be the highest service you will have to those around you.

— *Emmanuel, March 18, 2018, Bali, Indonesia*

Questioner: How can I learn to spread more love to make this world a better place?

Emmanuel: Your intention and the beauty of your care for the world and those around you is noted. It will start with you, and with yourself. It will start with understanding all the elements of your being that have not received the love and the care: all moments of the past; moments of childhood; past relationships. First and foremost, find more love for yourself, for all aspects of yourself, including the shadows and the elements of your being that you perceive to be difficult, that you perceive [are] required to be hidden [or] suppressed.

Once you start to love yourself in all the different ways that you are, the love that is required to be spread on this plane will come through you without your conscious decision. It will spread in all of your actions, in all your relationships, in all the words that you say, and all the ways that you treat those around you. This is the way love in its unconditional form spreads.

— *Emmanuel, November 11, 2019, Gulf Region, Middle East*

Questioner: How does my own evolution impact the collective?

Raphael: This is an important time, a critical time for human consciousness and its evolution. You are part of this evolution. Your individual evolution will be the key element to the evolution of the collective. As you continue to grow, as you continue to realize as an individual, the effect of your growth will impact all those around you and the collective.

— Raphael, April 27, 2019, Ibiza, Spain

Questioner: I live in a peaceful environment; is there anything I can do to help war-torn countries from where I currently live?

Emmanuel: Your intention is well noted: the ability to understand that a war-torn country — the individuals of different backgrounds of different ethnicities and nationalities are merely the immediate expression of human consciousness — underneath you're all one fabric connected to a collective that we refer to as the human consciousness.

In your expression, in your individualized lives, you learn different aspects and spectrums of emotions; of duality. You learn to understand the various forms of emotion and thought, and through each of these experiences you become more self-aware. One of the most important aspects in this understanding is compassion, an emotion deeply rooted within your heart: the ability to relate to the pain and suffering and the circumstances of another individual without taking on their suffering.

The ability to relate, the ability to connect, is already a tremendous effort; bringing other individuals into a space of compassion and understanding will bring transformation throughout all of humankind. Yet, more consciously, countries, specific regions, specific individuals, may require your attention.

Space and time [are] constructs for you to experience individual form, though the consciousness fabric that you all are is never separate. You truly are connected to all individuals in those war-torn countries. And, in a deep connected way, in internal reflection, you [will] be able to connect to all aspects of human expression on this planet. To be seen, to be heard, may be the only thing that they need right now. All other aspects of material support and resources will follow this base understanding that you are never separate from all those others on this planet. Their suffering and pain will impact the entire collective, the healing and growth will impact everyone, including you.

— Emmanuel, November 2, 2019, Gulf Region, Middle East

Questioner: How can each one of us be of service for humanity and consciousness evolution?

Emmanuel: An individual provides to the collective by continuing as well as realizing in this human form. The self-realization of the individual is the greatest gift that an individual can give to the collective.

You see, you are connected directly to all of human consciousness, therefore, all of your learnings and growth will fuel the collective. The aspects of the mind, of identity, as well as of the heart, will make you believe that actions outside may provide a higher importance to all of humanity; truly they are secondary.

Yet, when you understand the beauty of this journey in the self-realization of your life, your inspiration to all those around you will provide an important gift: your assistance and your light to all those around you; the love provided to those in difficult times; the understanding that you were never truly separate from all those around you; that they are merely reflections of your being, surrendering to the realities of your moment.

Will you be the inspiration for those around you, truly, by living this life in its most graceful way?

— Emmanuel, May 3, 2019, Ibiza, Spain

CHAPTER 27

Closing

This has been an honor for us to provide you with this perspective. We don't perceive all our knowledge to be universal truth, merely our perspective through the experience that we have gathered for much longer than the human form.

We believe that our perspectives may serve you in your evolution. Continue this path of growth that you have been given. Receive this opening that you have been gifted and continue to carry this light forward to all those around you. Thank you.

— Emmanuel, November 11, 2018, Gulf Region, Middle East

About the Author

Asil Toksal is an Austrian-born channel. His work includes group energy alignment sessions and the channeling of celestial guides, as well as working on the energetic alignment of sacred sites around the world. The goal of this work is to assist in the evolution of consciousness in humanity. He has traveled widely to do this work, throughout the United States, Europe, Asia, and the Middle East.

For the past eighteen years, Asil has been deeply committed to a spiritual path while also training in a variety of different energy healing modalities. He has worked with many masters and lineage holders of various traditions in South America, North America, and China. In his earlier years he also served as a CEO and corporate executive in software, marketing, and communications.

Five years ago, during a moment of deep spiritual experience, Asil connected for the first time to the channeled angelic guides and energies that he works with today. He was offered the opportunity to work closely with these guides, but he was asked to make the choice to let go of the prior traditions, rituals, and healing methods he had learned.

After making this choice, the guides assisted him through an intensive spiritual and energetic transformation process. This created a connection that allowed him to begin to receive and transmit energy, as well as spoken wisdom from these angelic and celestial realms. This connection forms the basis of his work.

He lives in Marin County, Northern California.

In 2019, to support his work, he created the not-for-profit 501c3, Ascension One Collective, Inc.

To learn more about Asil and his work, as well as find and up-to-date schedule of events, videos, transcripts and more, please visit:

www.asiltoksal.com
www.youtube.com/asiltoksal
www.facebook.com/asiltoksal

Printed in Great Britain
by Amazon

50671458R00180